Peter Young:
Ski for Life

Dave Barker

PublishNation
www.publishnation.co.uk

Dedicated to the memory of the best friend, training partner and mentor anyone could wish for.

Contents

Foreword

Peter was probably one of the best all-round sportsmen I have ever known. He competed in seven winter Paralympics in his best-loved sport, cross country skiing.

Not being content with this, he competed in the 1984 summer Paralympics and finished fourth in the 1500 metres in New York the other event he competed in plagued him for life I believe and will not be mentioned by me. As he was phenomenally fit, he decided to add tandem racing to his amazing sporting repertoire and competed in the European Championships in Zurich in 1989.

In the 1970's he played football for Metro and if international football had been played then, he would certainly have been selected for his country in that sport as well.

Most in the UK however would have met up with Peter on the cricket pitch. His outstanding fielding, and batting was a major asset for Metro over a 30-year period, as was his bowling during the latter years of his life. This helped Metro to remain at the top of the UK visually impaired cricket world.

And what of the man? Most will remember Peter for his guts, determination, massive competitive drive and for his will to win. He was fearless in the ski tracks, a formidable opponent both feared and respected by his competitors. I, however, will remember him for his friendship, sense of fun, capacity for drinking pints of anything alcoholic and sheer vitality. He was a born fighter, from his early life until the end.

Peter was given the Pery award for people who had made an outstanding contribution to the world of winter sport and exploration. Previous winners had been Sir Ranulph Feinnes, and the skier Martin Bell. He is proof that visual impairment is not a disability if the mind and will is strong enough to overcome it, it then becomes merely another challenge to beat.

The words used during the Pery award ceremony to describe Peter, probably sum up what I, friends in and outside of the Metro sports club, and the rest of the visually impaired sporting world would say about Peter.

"He was an outstanding sportsman, an outstanding human being and one hell of a guy"

Mike Brace CBE DL

Acknowledgements

I never thought that sitting writing something that happened so long ago would be as hard as it has been over the last 24 months. I guess that the entire period I ran with Peter set lasting impressions on me, and these have remained deeply ingrained within the fibres of who I was, who I became, and ultimately who I am today.

That said, without a lot of help, encouragement and persuasion I would never have got as far as I have, and Peter's story would have remained within me, untold, and unknown to the many who never had the pleasure of meeting him.

First, I would like to thank Mike Brace for his memories and for the huge amount of knowledge that he was able to pass on to me regarding the earlier years of Peter's life. This knowledge and the experiences he recalled shed light on a very patchy area of Peter's history, without which I would never have been able to complete this text. Mike, the work you have done for British blind sport has been immense, and everyone involved in and affected by it will reap the rewards of the hard work that you have done in the past, through today and into the future.

I must also thank James Brown for the information he gave me regarding Pete's early years on skis. I have met James in the past and the name is very familiar, though sadly I do not remember the face. I aim to rectify this as soon as is physically possible at some stage in the near future.

My thanks also to Dag and Lyder for their memories and for some of the pictures that are enclosed in the book. Strange to think that I ran with Peter for nearly half my life, yet only have a handful of pictures of us together. A picture paints a thousand words they say, and I hope that the pictures enclosed within the pages of this book help to convey the kind of fun-loving, yet deadly serious man Peter was.

To Geoff and Janice Thompson, it's been a long, long time since we spoke and for you to remember Peter in the detail you do is testament only to the kind of impression, he made on those around him. I thank you for your kind words, all of which were gratefully received and used where appropriate.

To Glen and Julie Moulds, wow, what an experience both good and bad arranging and completing the Karatethon was. I would never have believed it possible, and to rearrange a famous speech by Churchill "Never was so much owed by so few to so many" Other than writing this text, I think that was likely the most epic experience of my life. It was amazing, so thank you for thinking of the idea and bringing it to life.

On a more 'technical' l note, I would like to express my thanks to Mark for his input on the medical side of things, having a doctor in your corner checking the medical facts has been so very important. It's also helped me gain an understanding and belief that there really was nothing I could do and has maybe helped dispel one of the demonic 'black dogs' that have followed me for years, and who has bitten me at vulnerable moments.

To my proof-reader Maureen, your thoughts, insight and skill at changing the odd phrase here and there for the good of the story was much appreciated. Sometimes a fresh pair of eyes and someone who knows how to use a thesaurus is just what's needed. I have no doubt the entire story is better for your input.

I also want to thank 'Pandora' for helping me rip the lid of the section of my mind that contained my demons from this time in my life. Being able to face and put demons to rest is something that is hard, something that everyone needs, but few have the strength to attempt. Doing it alone would have been nigh on impossible, so to those who stood firmly in my corner, and who were there to support in whatever way they could, I thank you.

My thanks also to everyone who donated in order to allow me to get the book published and for PublishNation for their professionalism and patience in helping me get this book finally out there. That's said a book with no cover would look kind of strange, so my deepest thanks go to Scott Gaunt for the countless designs he produced, and for not getting really annoyed when I kept adding to and changing bits of it. The finished design is spot on.

Finally, my thanks go out to Peter, Jimmy, Kenny, Mike and Peter Longgate for allowing me into your world and for helping to corrupt me over many years. Seeing the world of the visually impaired from the inside was something extremely humbling and I would not have missed it for the world. My only regret is that I never kept on with it after Peter's passing in 2002. For those of you no longer with us, I imagine you are still causing havoc wherever you are, and for those still breathing on this earth, I shall endeavour to reignite contact with you as soon as I can.

Introduction

The Olympics, the greatest sporting event on earth, is in the thoughts of every up-and-coming athlete in every country in the world: From the time they put on their first pair of spikes or throw their first javelin and decide to commit to the hard work needed over a long period of time. From the time they admit they are willing to accept the ups and downs that follow a career in sport; accept and are willing to be seen as selfish individuals whilst their career is flourishing and have one thing in their minds, winning the Olympic Games in their chosen event.

The prestige of winning the Olympic Games and representing their country in the biggest festival of athletics in the world overshadows that of winning the World Championships or for that matter anything else. Nothing else is important other than reaching the absolute pinnacle of sporting achievement.

The possibility of going into the Hall of Fame with the likes of the Olympic Greats, such as Jessie Owens, Sebastian Coe, Steve Ovett, Daley Thompson, and Carl Lewis to name but just a few of the world's finest athletes, provides such a driving force that people make that commitment, and want to live the dream.

Sadly, very few of those in top level competitive athletics today reach those dizzy heights of success. Some work hard, but do not have the raw talent needed to reach the very top. Others, the opposite, have the raw talent but are not willing to push beyond the pain barrier to become the best they can be.

Some do not have the right support apparatus around them in the way of coaches and clubs, and others are side-tracked by other things in life. Others just don't want it bad enough. Those who do make it to the very top are recognized and remembered, forever. The others fade somewhat into obscurity.

But there is another group of people who are all too often forgotten. There are many world-class athletes, maybe even in your hometown that you know nothing about: inconspicuous, quiet, maybe even slight recluses who do not make an issue out of who they are. These people blend into the community, go about their everyday life without issue. These people are disabled.

For the normal layman in the street, a disabled person is often stereotyped as a poor, less fortunate soul, who has a hard life through no fault of their own. If one asks people in the street to describe a disability or disabled person, they will, in a majority of cases, chose something very obvious: amputees, those confined to wheelchairs, and those who have a mental disability. But this is only part of the picture.

When we look into what a disability is, it is defined in the Cambridge Dictionary as 'not having one or more of the physical or mental abilities that most people have'. (1)

But a disability is also defined as an impairment that may be cognitive, developmental, intellectual, mental, physical, sensory, or some combination of these. It substantially affects a person's life activities and may be present from birth or occur at any stage during a person's lifetime.

The word disability is an umbrella term, covering impairments, activity limitations, and participation restrictions. An impairment is a problem in body function or structure; an activity limitation is a difficulty encountered by an individual in executing a task or action; while a participation restriction is a problem experienced by an individual in involvement in life situations. Disability is thus not just a health problem. It is a complex phenomenon, reflecting the interaction between features of a person's body and features of the society in which he or she lives. (2)

As we can see the scope and degree of what comprises a disability is wide ranging, particularly when most of those with a physical disability have adapted themselves over time and manage to take part in all aspects of society. In some situations, they manage far better than their 'able-bodied' counterparts do.

So, because a person is not as 'able-bodied' as someone else, does this mean they should not be afforded the same opportunities as those who have no disability? Should they not be allowed to compete in high-level sporting events? Even more so should they not be afforded the same level of respect, recognition and financial support as those able-bodied elite athletes we all know and love? To put it another way, would any of the all-time Olympic Greats hold the status they do now had they been disabled? I leave that for you to answer in the privacy of your own mind

Let's look at the London Marathon as an example (or any marathon for that matter). The wheelchair competitors are an amazing group of people. They are highly motivated, highly conditioned, and have incredible physical and mental strength and fitness. But this does not come for free. They train hard, they sacrifice, and they accept that they may be seen as selfish whilst their career flourishes, all of the same attributes that their able-bodied counterparts have. Are they a lesser athlete? Well try asking our own Olympic champion Mo Farah to sit in a wheelchair and race 10,000 metres against these guys. I can only imagine what his comments would be!

But sensory disabilities are possibly harder to define than the physical ones, and to go into much detail is possibly the theme for another type of story. Now we are looking at the world of the visually impaired. This in itself has different definitions within the definition. Different levels of visual impairment provide a wide range of challenges, which in many cases vary from person to person.

Some people look at the disability as nothing more than something that has to be lived with; others decide at some stage of their lives that they want to show the world that they are no more disabled because they may not be able to see properly, than you, the reader.

One of these people was Peter Young, a piano tuner by trade, yet an awe-inspiring and highly respected competitor in the world of blind sport. Not just in one area though. Peter competed internationally in track athletics, participating in the New York Summer Paralympics, in World and European Cycling Championships, and in his true and ultimate love, Nordic skiing inclusive biathlons, (yes you read correctly, the man skied then shot a rifle with live rounds). He competed internationally over a span of over 20 years with his first Paralympics in Toronto, Canada in 1976 aged 20. His final Paralympics were in Nagano, Japan in 1998. His retirement was caused by one race against a formidable opponent. A race he was not going to win. His Ski for Life.

Was he any good is the next question? Well everything is relative, but winning Olympic bronzes, World and European Championship golds and the King of Norway Cup would be seen as a successful career in the 'able–bodied' world, so, taking into account that he won all of these, I guess we can conclude that yes, he was good.

Peter touched the lives of everyone he met in some way or another. From the schoolchildren he met during his normal working day, to Royalty. Once you had met Peter Young at his best (or worst depending on what he did and how you viewed it) your life was never going to be the same again. Ever! The impression he made on you was indelible.

My role in all of this is simple. I was privileged enough to meet Peter when I was 17 and started guiding him through the streets of our home borough of Barking and Dagenham in Essex. It started out as mutual assistance with each other's training and developed into a long-lasting and completely unique relationship that affected us both in many ways. It is fair to say that my life was changed forever, and in some ways shaped, by the time I spent with Peter. Peter died in 2002; this is his story, to best of my ability.

1

The Early Years

In the mid-1950s, over the course of 18 months, three outstanding and inspirational people were born, destined to change the course of British athletics in the years to come. Two of these quickly became household names from the mid-1970s until their retirement over a decade later, and it is difficult to mention one in a sentence without mentioning the other. Their names were Steve Ovett, born in Brighton in October 1955 and Sebastian Coe, born in Sheffield in September 1956. These two men shared championships and world records throughout the entire 1980's, winning Olympic, World, Commonwealth and European Championship medals and titles, and putting themselves in the history books forever.

But there was a third, born a few months after Ovett and some months before Coe in January 1956. A man born into a working-class family in Dagenham, Essex, who never became a household name; in fact, it is true to say that whilst you the reader have undoubtedly heard of the first two, you would likely never have heard of the last.

He never set world records. He rarely featured in the media, but his story is one that has inspired many, in just the same way as Coe and Ovett. He too set a very clear mark on the world of British athletics, but in his case, it was in the field of blind winter sports and he paved the way for the luxury of support and sponsorship that today's blind elite are able to enjoy.

On Monday 16th January, in 1956 in a small terraced council house in Dagenham Essex, Joan Young, a part time carer at a local old people's home, and her husband, Ford factory worker Sidney Young, sat and ate their evening meal, just like any other normal evening.

Then things started to happen Joan started to feel the familiar pains of labour; they were soon to have their second child.

They already had one son, Paul, and a few hours later he was the proud older brother of another little boy, whom they named Peter Sidney Young.

There is nothing special about a family increasing in size, or in them having two sons, but this second child was destined for great things, despite there being some worrying and heart-breaking times in the first short years of his life. He was a happy–go-lucky boy, who was developing a sense for mischief as he grew. However, shortly after his second birthday his parents noticed something was wrong, and the resulting doctors' appointments, tests and follow-ups gave the news that all parents must dread more than anything – Peter had cancer.

In mid-1958, aged just over 2 years old, Peter was diagnosed with retinoblastoma and his parents were faced with an agonizing decision. One which truly was that of life and death, and although many might see the answer as simple, it was something that posed problems of its own in the late 1950s.

Cancer starts when cells begin to grow out of control. Cells in nearly any part of the body can become cancerous and can spread to other areas of the body. Retinoblastoma is a cancer that starts in the retina, the very back part of the eye.

The eyes develop very early as the baby grows in the womb. During the early stages of development, the eyes have cells called retinoblasts that divide into new cells and fill the retina. At a certain point, these cells stop dividing and develop into mature retinal cells. However, and fortunately only rarely, something goes wrong with this process. Instead of maturing into special cells that detect light, some retinoblasts continue to divide and grow out of control, forming a cancer known as retinoblastoma. It is the most common type of eye cancer in children and is caused by a mutation in the so-called retinoblastoma (RB1) gene. The retinoblastoma gene is called a tumour suppressor gene, as it is responsible for producing a protein that helps control cell division (and so stop or 'suppress' the development of a tumour). If the gene is 'faulty' (mutated), then the cell is more prone to becoming cancerous. One mutation in the gene may not be sufficient to cause the cell to become cancerous but means that if a second mutation were to occur (as often happens in cells), it is far more likely that the cell will become cancerous. Sometimes, a mutation in the retinoblastoma gene is inherited, making it far more likely that retinoblastoma will develop. As the mutation is present in all the body cells, these individuals are also at greater risk of developing other malignant growths in the future. In other cases, the mutation is not inherited, but develops anew, or 'de novo', during early development in the womb. This is sometimes referred to as 'sporadic' retinoblastoma.

Recent statistics (2017–2018) show that 1 out of 3 children with retinoblastoma have the abnormality present at birth and it is found in all the cells of the body, including all the cells of both retinas. In most affected children, there is no family history of this cancer; only about 25% of the children born with this genetic mutation inherit it from a parent. In about 75% of children the gene change first occurs during early development in the womb. The reasons for this are not clear even today.

Children born with this genetic mutation usually develop retinoblastoma in both eyes and there are often several tumours within the eye. Retinoblastoma cells can occasionally spread to other parts of the body. The cells sometimes grow along the optic nerve and reach the brain. Retinoblastoma cells can also grow through the covering layers of the eyeball and into the eye socket, eyelids and nearby tissues. Once the cancer reaches tissues outside the eyeball, it can then spread to lymph nodes (small bean-shaped collections of immune system cells) and to other organs such as the liver, bones and bone marrow (the soft, inner part of many bones). This was the case with

Peter, both eyes developing tumours which untreated would definitely have cost him his life at a very early stage.

Treatment options for retinoblastoma have not changed that drastically since the 1950s, but the treatments available were not as advanced as they are today, and Peter's condition narrowed the options further. His parents were then faced with a very difficult decision.

Today's treatments now depend on the size of the tumour. If it is small, then so-called local therapy – laser therapy, freezing therapy (called cryotherapy) or heating therapy (thermotherapy) – can be used; sometimes these are followed by chemotherapy. Chemotherapy can sometimes be given first to try and shrink a larger tumour to make it then possible to use one of the local therapies.

Radiotherapy can also be used, sometimes with a tiny radioactive plate stitched in place over the tumour for a length of time (this is called brachytherapy) or given as 'external beam' radiotherapy to the whole eye. The more invasive treatment surgery to remove the eye is done when it is clear that there is no function left in the eye (usually for larger tumours).

Retinoblastoma is extremely rare, with only around 45 children being diagnosed each year in the UK. The cure rate is very high (for cancer) at around 90% or thereabouts. The main difference between now and the 1950s is not the cure, but that the treatment is less disabling although just as effective. (3)

Questions ran through Joan and Sid's minds. How would Peter cope with being blind? How would they, the family, cope with Peter being blind, and what adjustments would be needed to assist a legally disabled child? In addition, what support apparatus was available for them at that time? The infrastructure in the1950s was still poor in this regard. There was little help available, so the family set about the task of finding out what they needed to know.

The best course of treatment for Peter was deemed to be surgical removal of his eyes followed by radiation treatment. Peter's eyes were removed. He was now blind and faced a childhood where he would be subjected to the sympathy and condescension that at that time were common when dealing with the disabled. Peter remembered very little of being sighted. As I recall his one memory is that of a brown dog.

A short while later the Young family grew a bit more; another boy was born and named David. The period during David's first few years were hard for his parents with a blind toddler in the house and the constant worry that maybe their third child would develop cancer in the same manner as Peter had. Joan and Sid were strong and faced this time in the only manner they knew how: by knuckling down and doing the best as was possible for their children given the fateful hand of cards they had been dealt.

By all intents and purposes Peter never really suffered too much by not being included in the activities of other children. In the cul-de-sac in which they lived there were several other families with young children, and one of these, Derek Coates, became firm friends with Peter and was to play a large role in his athletics and sporting career some years later.

One thing that was never affected throughout his early illness, was Peter's sense of fun and mischief; he was in essence a normal little boy, growing up with two brothers and doing the things that little boys do. His other senses improved as a result of losing his sight, and as several people noted later in his life, it really was almost impossible to notice that Peter was blind.

The worse thing that you could ever do was tell Peter he was disabled. His answer was very simple, but sadly not something that is printable!

LINDEN LODGE AND FRIENDS

When Peter turned six in 1962, he started at a boarding school for the visually impaired in Wandsworth, and later moved on to the main school site in Wimbledon. Linden Lodge School for the Blind is a specialist sensory and physical college located in south London. It educates visually impaired children aged between two and nineteen, including those who are multi-disabled, and visually impaired. The school was one of two residential schools for blind children opened by the London School Board in 1902. Initially for boys only, but as demand grew girls also being admitted, the original location of the school was at Wandsworth Common. The present main school building was designed by the architect Sir Edwin Lutyens in 1934.

Peter lived at the school during the school week and returned home each weekend. He was a boisterous lad and as he grew and developed, he used his blindness and his glass eyes to his advantage. He earned 10 pence a time for taking his eye out in front of friends and was nicknamed Boris after the horror actor Boris Karloff. It was at Linden Lodge that Peter learnt about being blind, and, in particular, about the challenges that blindness would cause in regard to mobility. He also learnt how to read and write Braille.

Braille is the written language used by all visually impaired people throughout the world, and is named after its creator, Louis Braille, a Frenchman who lost his sight as a result of a childhood accident. In 1824, at the age of fifteen, he developed a code for the French alphabet as an improvement on the earlier 'night writing' created during the Napoleonic wars of the early 1800s, when Napoleon had demanded that French soldiers should communicate silently in darkness, without the use of a light source. He published his system, which subsequently included musical notation, in 1829. The second revision, published in 1837, was the first small binary form of writing developed in the modern era.

These characters have rectangular blocks called cells that have tiny bumps called raised dots. The number and arrangement of these dots distinguish one character from another. Since the various Braille alphabets originated as transcription codes for printed writing, the mappings (sets of character designations) vary from language to language, and even within one; in English Braille there are three levels of encoding: Grade 1 – a letter-by-letter transcription used for basic literacy; Grade 2 – an addition of abbreviations and contractions; and Grade 3 – various non-standardized personal stenography. Although there are a few exceptions, sighted people struggle to read Braille with their fingers, the way in which the visually impaired read. The reason for this is unknown, though it is suspected that due to having sight, the eyes take some of the focus away from what the fingers are feeling.

It was also at Linden Lodge that Peter met two of the many people who were to become lifelong friends: Mike Brace, who was to be instrumental in setting Peter on the path to becoming an athlete, and Jimmy Denton. Jimmy the same age as Peter was partially sighted.

Mike was six years senior but had not been at the school much longer than Peter. He became partially sighted after holding a glass bottle containing a lighted firework when he was aged 11; the firework went off and caused the bottle to explode covering Mike in glass and damaging his eyes. Although this did not blind him, it rendered him partially sighted, Mike never started at Linden Lodge until a year or so after the accident, his blindness the result of retinal haemorrhaging caused by trying to play the trumpet at school. Mike and Peter became firm friends even at an early age and with a six-year age gap between them.

Mike went on to become a social worker and head of several disabled charities. He was Chief Executive of Vision 2020 UK (2001– 2012) and served as Chairman of the British Paralympic Association (2001–2008). He gained a Diploma in Social Work from the Polytechnic of North London in 1976 and was the subject of This Is Your Life in 1982. He was later awarded the OBE and the CBE

Although very intelligent, Peter was generally a lazy student, who needed challenges and constant stimulation in order to get on with his schoolwork. He enjoyed having fun and was rather rebellious. Even at a young age Peter was impatient. Learning Braille takes time, and Peter was in a hurry to finish each day; schoolwork was far too time-consuming, so he opted to take short cuts and used a Dictaphone instead. In time, he did naturally learn to read and write Braille, but even in his adult years preferred the Dictaphone and carried one constantly in his bag wherever he went.

Peter was never a tall child, standing only around 5 feet 8 inches as an adult, and his growth development was late. This saw him cast as one of the seven dwarfs in the school play. It was not something that he ever made public and not something he was particularly happy speaking about in later years. But during after-ski parties and other social events it was something that was often bought up, much to Peter's dismay.

As time passed Peter developed into a typical teenage boy and developed a taste for both beer and girls. Linden Lodge was not a school segregated into boys and girls, and Peter developed friendships with many people of both sexes. One such friendship led to him being expelled for a short period of time in the early 1970s. I do not have all of the details, and to be honest I am quite thankful not to sit here with such detailed information, but it was after a class towards the end of the day that Peter and his younger girlfriend were caught literally with their pants down in the music room by a teacher. Peter being the older of the two was deemed the instigator (though whether this is the case or not I cannot speculate) and he was expelled.

Peter's biggest issue with the schooling at Linden Lodge during his time there was the lack of training the students received in regard to mobility. Being blind and navigating your way through busy streets and even through familiar surroundings is challenging when your primary sense is removed. We have all played blind man's bluff as children, being blindfolded and trying to find friends without being able to see them. It is not something that is easy by any means and having to live constantly in a world without sight is, at least for me, a daunting thought. Peter believed that in order for the blind and visually impaired to be able to function properly, mobility should have had a much higher focus in their education. Indeed, it is this that many struggles within the real world.

The training they received did not include the use of the long cane that is stereotypically associated with the blind. There are three types of canes that are used by the visually impaired. The first is very short and known as the symbol cane. This is, as the name suggests, just a white cane that in essence has little or no practical use other than giving a signal to those around them that the person carrying it is visually impaired. The second, longer cane is known as the guide cane and reaches from the hip to the ground. This is predominantly used by those who are either partially sighted or who have conditions that mean their sight is impeached in the dark or in periods of fog or other bad weather. Its use is simply that of keeping the user in contact with the ground at all times and warning of any deviation in level. Most totally blind people use the long cane. This cane can be solid, but modern times have seen it made into a collapsible cane that can be stowed in bags when not needed. It reaches from the sternum to the floor and is used in addition to the use of sound to ensure that any obstacles are identified and avoided as soon as possible, as well as symbolising to those around that the person is visually impaired. During his time at school Peter only received training in using a much shorter version.

Prior to graduation all students needed to pass a number of tests. The tests were designed to show that the students were able to navigate themselves in a world of noise and other people, and in situations that were not as controlled as they were in school. These included walking around the block and taking bus and train rides.

The blind world is based on other senses. The sense of touch is vitally important, but the sense most used is that of sound. Having spent a lot of time immersing myself in the world of the blind and visually impaired, it is fair to say that sound is the single most important sense that needs to be developed. It is also true that other senses are heightened by the loss of another. However, the system most blind people use in order to navigate was not taught or touched upon at the school. The system is formally known as Human

Echolocation but is more commonly called the sound shadow and is used all day every day by the visually impaired to orientate themselves in a room, and to identify the positions of a wall, a window or a door. This was something that Peter and his friends had to develop for themselves. It was not taught at the school and both Peter and Mike were critical of this omission in their training.

The majority of visually impaired people are skilled at echolocating silent objects simply by producing mouth clicks and listening to the returning echoes. The object which returns the echo will have differing densities and this sound will, with experience, tell the listener what kind and size the object is, and its position in the room or area. The sound shadow can really only be described as a form of human sonar and must be compared to the way that bats orientate and navigate around in the darkness. Peter's skill level was nothing short of incredible, and this must be put down to it being developed instinctively through becoming blind at such an early age. None the less there was little or no focus on this during their schooling and it was something they felt was lacking in order for them to cope in the real world.

Peter finished his schooling at Linden Lodge in 1974 aged 18 and went on to train as a piano tuner in Shoreditch in east London. His heightened senses allowed him to excel at this trade, and he was able to help others in his class finish their work early so that they could get to their lunchtime rendezvous at the local pub in good time each day. All the group were of a similar age and it was at Shoreditch that Peter met Kenny Bodden who had also lost his sight due to cancer. Together they were a formidable gang: Kenny, extroverted with a loud disposition, who fed off Peter's immense energy, and the slightly more subdued Jimmy whose quick wit and dry humour complimented that of the other two. The three became good friends and saw them travel the world in the name of sport for decades after their first meeting. Sadly, Kenny passed a few short years ago; Jimmy still competes and trains whilst working as a piano tuner in Berkshire.

The drinking and high life were, however, taking their toll on Peter. He was not a smoker, but he was never one to partake in any form of serious exercise other than the walk to the pub. He lived unhealthily, eating fast foods and curry as a staple part of his diet and his weight climbed into the range of obesity.

Mike Brace by this time had met a young lady named Maureen, and they married in 1972. Pete was at this time 16 and had been firm friends with Mike since they had met 10 years before at school. He attended Mike's stag night at a pub in the Victoria area of London and he tried to show those around him that, although he may only be 16 in age, he could drink as much as the next man. Peter, however, was not a man who had a high threshold before feeling the effects of alcohol.

Mike recalls:

> There was quite a group of us, and after the initial drinking started people just kept buying round after round of drinks. At one stage I am sure there were 3 or 4 on the table in front of Peter and even though he was falling behind, he never said no when asked if he wanted a drink, and never had a problem putting his hand in his pocket and taking his turn.
>
> As the evening progressed, he got more and more drunk. He was in a real state but refused flat out to go home and tried desperately to keep up. At that stage it was not so much that he was not a big drinker, but more that he drank slower than the rest of us. You have to remember he was 6 or more years our junior.
>
> As was the case more often back then it was not unusual for a landlord to have a lock in (continue drinking and taking payment outside of normal licencing hours) and Peter was still there to the bitter end. He was extremely

drunk, and I don't remember how he got home, or in fact if he got home that night.

Prior to the increase in his weight Peter had played a little sport for the London Sports club, and in 1973 Peter, Mike Brace, Alan Mayber, Keith Wells and a man named Graham Salmon, all of whom had attended Linden Lodge, decided they would start their own sports club, that would cover the entire metropolitan area and not just that of London. For the cost of five pounds a head the Metro London Sports Club was born. It later changed its name to just Metro and is now seen as Britain's largest sports club for the visually impaired.

Peter took part in some of the events, more through obligation than desire, and at a competition based at Stoke Mandeville in late 1973 the boys from Metro hauled a total of 48 medals, despite only numbering 8 or 9 people. Peter had the bug for sport, but training was far too much of an effort and he took things as they came, never really being concerned as to whether he won, lost or drew.

Things changed in the late winter of 1973 when Mike and the Metro sports club were contacted by a man named Dave Adams. Dave had managed to secure 15 places skiing in Norway and wondered if there was any interest at the club for cross-country skiing.

Mike recalls the incident fondly:

> In 1973 Dave Adams, who was a social worker for Brent Council I think, contacted me as Chair of the newly formed Metro Sports Club to see if I and some of my members would be interested in trying cross-country skiing.
>
> I of course said yes and recruited a bunch of visually impaired skiers to try it out, one of which was an 18-year-old, 16 stone heavy, Peter.

He was overweight and Dave Adams, the leader of the group, was rather surprised that he was there if the truth be known. We stayed in a bed and breakfast type accommodation and the living was very spartan meaning a shared bathroom for 14 people and very basic rooms.

At that time cross-country skiing was not really televised. The general misconception was that skiing was alpine downhill skiing, Franz Klammer style. Peter was one of those who expressed an interest and to Beitostølen in eastern Norway he went. There was no real idea as to what to expect at that time, and Peter had decided that the skiing was the secondary reason for being there. It was a necessary evil needing to be done in order to get to the main event, the after-ski partying.

Mike recalls:

We arrived in Beitostølen without any idea as to what cross-country skiing was or how we did it. It was kind of exciting; almost like a new lease of life. It was something we could do without any risk of getting lost. The tracks were prepared, there was not too much downhill involved and we had no idea of the technique required. Besides it was our first time, so we were not going exactly fast.

Peter on the other hand was really only interested in the after-ski and the Scandinavian ladies. In fact, I seem to remember that his ski bag contained a couple of party 7 beer cans (a can holding 7 pints) more than it held any skiing equipment.

The trip to Norway had, however, had one effect. Peter had found something in the world of sport that he loved. It had awoken a passion in him that he never knew he had, and although he never took it too seriously it was something that he wanted to do again. The year of 1974 was a poignant time in his life and saw him start to take part in more and more sport. He registered his interest as a more active member of the Metro sports club joining the cricket and football teams as well.

To those without knowledge of blind sport it may seem impossible to play such sports as cricket and football without being able to see. These games were not new to the world of the visually impaired and were played with normal balls that contained metal ball bearings. Each time the ball moved the bearings made a noise allowing the players to locate it. The rules of the games are slightly different in order to accommodate the lack of sight.

Over the next couple of years, the Metro sports club continued to grow in stature and Mike was re-elected Chairman. Although there was no media focus on blind sport at that time, Mike and Metro were invited, as the only sports club for visually impaired athletes, to select a team for a skiing competition to be held in Sweden in 1976. This was the beginning of the Winter Paralympics, and the inaugural games saw the start of a change in Peter. Mike recalls: 'I managed to beat Peter at those first games, but that experience spurred us on to ski each year and then to attend the trials for the 1976 first Winter Paralympics.'

Training started and the selection process was held at the military base in Aldershot under the watchful eye of Lieutenant Colonel John Moore. A specially made cross-country ski track was installed. It was made of plastic and was approximately 1,500 metres in length. There were no guides available at this time making the training and selection process a little more difficult. Peter, Mike as well as a few others made weekly trips to Aldershot, banking on the tractors and cars being placed across each end of the ski track in order stop them. They also relied heavily on the use of the sound shadow; the one thing that had never been taught whilst they were at school, but which proved to be vitally important.

The British team were poorly prepared for the games in Sweden. They had no access to snow, had no real guides, and their equipment was not like that of countries where skiing was a normal part of winter life. They turned up in plastic shell suits. The guides and athletes had no time to prepare together, and the event was a shamble in regard to the British team. Mike was guided into a barrier during the first event and never finished, and Peter was last in all three events in which he took part. Peter's competitive nature rose its head and he was determined to do better next time.

At this stage Pete was still somewhat rebellious and was warned by the British team that he had to be on his best behaviour and not cause the kind of mayhem that tended to follow him. He still had a love affair with beer and his weight was 16 stones (224 pounds or 101 kilograms).

The British team had caught the attention of the BBC. Mike remembers:

They were in touch and wanted to film for *This Week*. They filmed for a while covering Pete with his dad Sid at the greyhound racing in Romford, and also all of us skiing at the games. Funny thing is Pete was warned to watch his language when filming as he swore like a trooper then, and the only one to be caught swearing on camera was me!

Peter's weight was beginning to be a problem. It was pointed out to him in a rather offensive manner one evening after racing when Mike along with some of the other team members and guides were relaxing in the hotel pool. Pete emerged from the changing rooms dressed only in swimming trunks, and a comment was made as he jumped in the pool that he resembled Moby Dick. It was the first time that Peter had taken any notice of his increasing waistline and weight, and he decided that it was time to do something about it. The nickname of Moby Dick or just Moby was used fondly towards him by his close circle of friends for many years.

After returning home from the inaugural Paralympics in 1976, Peter decided he needed to focus on getting fit. This in turn would help reduce his weight. He cut back on alcohol and the amount of food that he ate and slowly started training in any way he could. He became more active in the sporting events held by Metro and also started cycling on a stationary cycle. The effect of the training materialized quickly and when he returned to Beitostølen in 1977 he was several stone lighter and more focused on the training. Sadly, though, skiing was still second priority to the after-ski sessions and womanizing he loved so much in the evenings.

Unexpected help come to the British team in 1977 via a Norwegian named Rolf Wilhelmsen. He had found a fund that had laid dormant for over a decade that he knew Mike Brace would be extremely interested in.

Mike knew Rolf through a mutual friend, Jan Knutsen, who acted as Peter's guide in the inaugural Paralympics and for some years afterwards. Rolf was a trustee of the Anglo-Norse fund founded in 1953 after dreadful floods in Newcastle, England. The floods caused immense damage with water levels rising to record high levels, only surpassed by the North Sea floods nearly 60 years later. The Norwegians had given aid to Britain during this time and the fund that was established was used to assist in funding housing repairs and food until such times that families could once again support themselves.

Rolf had used this fund in order to send Norwegian Athletes to the 1977 Metro games (an event hosted by Metro every year), and after some discussion it was decided by the fund committee that as long as the monies were used in order to support co-operation and friendship between the two countries then the British team could also reap the benefits of the monies that were available.

This saw the British athletes receive subsidies in regard to travel. It paid entry to the Ridderrennet event held in Beitostølen each year and gave a 25% discount on hotels. This amount has risen to 50% in later years and the Anglo-Norse fund is still a major supporter of the British skiing team.

The Ridderrennet is the original 'Ski for light' event that is now held all over the world. Norwegian Erling Størdal was the founder of the event in the early 1960s.

Størdal was himself blind but decided that cross-country skiing was an ideal sport for the visually impaired as the tracks in the snow provided a way of guiding the skier, theoretically meaning that they were not totally dependent on having a guide with them. He raised money throughout Norway, enough to build the sports and therapy centre at Beitostølen, which has grown as a national centre of excellence, and where some of the international cross-country skiing events are held each year.

The British team now had huge opportunities to train on snow and compete in skiing events that they had only ever dreamed of before. Mike and Peter became inspired, and by 1980 the training had become serious. A small group met at Mike's house several times a week in order to use weights and a treadmill, in order to run and gain fitness. The Norwegians provided guides when requested in order to allow skiing trips to take place and the bond between the British team and their Norwegian counterparts went from strength to strength.

2

Now It's Serious

The funding that had been given, coupled with a much higher level of motivation, saw Peter compete seriously in his first ski competition in Geilo, Norway, in 1980. We must remember that this was a man who earlier would have rather sat drinking than break into a sweat; someone who had never really applied himself to anything in his life before; a man nicknamed Moby by his friends, who had weighed 16 stones and who stood only 5 feet 8 inches tall.

In 1980 at Geilo in Norway the man that had been Peter was gone. He had been replaced by someone who had applied himself to changing his lifestyle, not just in the way that he looked but also in his entire attitude to competing. Prior to this change, the after-ski had always been the main event, and the skiing just a bonus of the trip. Standing on the start line now was the same person, but now weighing 13 stone and believing they really could be good at this.

He was right. The event he competed in was a 20-kilometre classic race (almost like running on skis), and despite it being extremely hard Pete exhibited a trait that no one, not even himself, knew he possessed. He had a dogged determination, the bit was firmly between his teeth, he was not going to stop, not going to give up and was going to push with everything he had. This trait is displayed by all of the world's elite athletes and it is this ability to be able to continue pushing hard when it hurts the most that differentiates the good from the exceptional.

He finished in an impressive 10th place. His success fed his desire to succeed further, and it was now Peter's real self that came to the fore. He had found something that he liked, something he was good at, and something he wanted to be the best in the world at doing. He returned home to Dagenham after the trip in 1980 inspired with a single-mindedness in becoming the best.

The results from the British team filtered slowly through to the realms of the British media, mainly due to Mike Brace's constant pressure, and, not long after, Waymark Holidays, a company specializing in holidays for those wanting to try cross-country skiing, made contact with him.

In their own way Waymark adopted the British disabled ski team, offering free training places at resorts such as Beitostølen and Geilo. The then Tour Leader for the company, Rosemary Crosby, contacted her Norwegian colleagues and put the word out that the British visually impaired ski team were serious, they were for real, and they were looking for Norwegian guides. Waymark still support the ski team today, nearly 40 years later, providing subsidies for travel and occasionally offering free flights for the sighted helpers who are an absolute necessity for the skiers.

In the meantime, there was work to be done and Peter started searching for a way to run at home. Treadmills were limited in their capabilities in the 80s and did not provide what was needed. Peter, Mike and some others continued training in the garage, and Mike was seeing Pete at least three times a week. It was around this time that Peter met a man named Gerry Madden who acted as Peters guide for a number of years. Gerry, a decent club level athlete in his own right though a little older than Peter, lived a little way away and managed to run with Peter a couple of times a week.

The benefits of extra training were obvious: Peter would get out in order to build the cardiovascular fitness he needed for his event, and in addition it would help him shed more of the extra weight that he was carrying.

Gerry guided Peter competitively until around 1984, when they competed in the Summer Paralympics in New York, details of which are covered later in this book. After these events they continued to run together for a number of years.

At this time Peter wanted more; the more training her could do the better. His old childhood friend Derek Coates who had lived in the same street as Pete was by this time a very accomplished athlete in his own right. He was a member of Ilford Athletics club, and was county champion as well as club record holder. It is my understanding that to this day some of these club records are still valid.

Derek and Peter started running a couple of days a week, and Peter's training went to another level. Running up to 4 days a week, and with additional cross-training by way of weights, etc., his fitness level reached new heights. His weight dropped further as well, increasing his motivation.

Team Peter, Derek and Gerry started finding races and testing themselves, not only against the visually impaired, but also against the able bodied, something that posed challenges for guides, especially in the larger events.

As Peter's confidence grew, and his fitness increased, it became necessary for his guides to plan training specific to exactly what Peter wanted and needed. Sometimes, however, this was difficult. Both Gerry and Derek competed as individuals as well, meaning that sometimes their needs were not the same as those that Peter had. Although there were never any real issues in this regard, it did mean that Peter sometimes might not have been able to focus on what he needed in order to become the best he could be.

In the early part of 1983 Peter met a man who was a font of all knowledge and who he would introduce me to some years later. The man was named John Sullivan, a national coach based at Mile End in London. He was a very humble man, from working-class roots, who had himself been a very high-level athlete in his youth. His training methods were not unlike those of Harry Wilson (coach to Steve Ovett) or those of Peter Coe (coach and father to Sebastian Coe), and he was more than willing to assist Peter in any way he could.

21

Peter, the willing athlete and even more willing student, took the sessions and information he received from John and developed his own training plans. On days when it was not possible for his guides to meet with him through other commitments, Peter would once more revert back to the treadmill and complete the sessions he had designed himself, based on John Sullivan's knowledge and suggestions. Peter was by this time a self-employed piano tuner which gave him the freedom to travel when he wanted, and more importantly whenever he wanted.

It was to pay dividends in the Winter Olympics of 1984 in Innsbruck, Austria, where Peter won a bronze medal, only 8 years after standing on skis for the first time; the boy once named Moby Dick by his friends was now lean, well trained and completely committed to achieving what he wanted to do, and nothing was going to stop him achieving it under any circumstance.

Peter was beaten in Innsbruck by two Norwegians, a man named Terje Løvås, and another named Magne Lunde. Innsbruck saw the start of a love/hate rivalry that brought out the best in all three men. It provided motivation to train more, to train harder, to train faster, in order to try to better the others. Unlike their professional counterparts in the world of sighted British sports, they did not receive the media coverage and there was no pre-event hype surrounding who had said what to whom. The love/hate conflict was simple: they loved being around each other after the events and were good and firm friends; they hated being beaten, by anyone.

Peter had nailed his colours firmly to the mast. He wanted to be the best in the world. He was pretty much in control of his training, other than some difficulties in managing to run as often as he wanted, owing to Derek competing himself, and Gerry often working and living away from where Peter was based. It meant that there were periods where he was left to his own devices in regard to fitness, and despite immense self-taught knowledge and knowledge gleaned from John Sullivan, there was only so much that was possible on treadmills.

Peter continued in this manner for some years until in 1986 when another long-term guiding relationship began. The British team of which Peter was a proud member was invited to a school in Gol, in Hallingdal, Norway in order to meet with guides and train. A student at the school was a partially blind Irishman named James Brown who was active in the world of cycling and went on to win Olympic gold. James himself competed in six Olympic Games (both Summer and Winter) and 22 World Championships in different events, including track running, triathlon, swimming, cycling and Nordic skiing.

Peter was introduced to two people who were willing to help out with guiding: a man who had previously guided James, Dag Olimbe, 9 years Peter's junior, and Trond Lundeshaug. The three of them trained together as often as they could. Guides were sparse so both Dag and Trond guided for others as well, including Jimmy Denton and Mike Brace. Peter had a more regular guide named, Jan Knutsen, who had taught him to ski in the first place.

Dag was born in 1965 and was currently finishing his schooling. He competed actively in both slalom, alpine, and cross-country skiing. He was almost the stereotype of the typical Norwegian man, large boned, muscular and light haired, and someone who had invariably been born with skis on his feet as per the adage often associated with the Norwegians. Neither Dag nor Trond saw Peter as disabled; they had met through a common interest and love of skiing, and even though Peter was not sighted and was technically not as gifted as some of those he would compete against in years to come he had heart, he had guts, and he had the resolve to never know when he was beaten. This dogged determination would remain with him until the end. It was soon recognized that Peter had potential to be a world beater and when training with him, everyone did their best to push him as best as they could.

James Brown has a clear recollection of Peter:

I met Pete in early April 1981 when I first attended the Ridderrennet in Beitostølen, Norway. I was 16 years old and this was my first experience of cross-country skiing. I had been training as a middle-distance runner for a couple of years at that time so took to my new activity well. After all they are very similar other than not really being able to lift your feet.

I was lucky to have a very strict guide who wanted nothing other than perfection, but that was not going to happen straight away. Of course, I wouldn't say my technique was anywhere near perfect but that was the standard to which we aspired together. We got on really well and enjoyed our time together. On the final day of the week's activities we took part in the famous Ridderrennet, a 15-20km mountain race which began with a fairly stiff up-hill section. With youth and fitness on my side I found myself pulling ahead of my guide on the climb and I remember him swearing at me, slightly regretting the standard of the training we had been given. But he caught up with me at the top and he got in front to guide me on the long descent that followed. I remember lots about that race to this day including the feelings, the weather, the speed, the hot juice we drank at the halfway point, the sheer exhaustion towards the end.

I think I finished quicker than every other British skier except Pete Young. That day he won my respect. I knew how hard I had worked in that race, harder than I'd ever done in any sporting event previously. I am partially blind, in class B2, and I knew that the 5% sight I did have gave me a significant advantage over those who had none, including Pete. The interaction between guide and skier is very different between those with partial sight and those who are totally blind. I'd only known Pete a few days by this point, but I knew enough to idolize him already!

I think it was on the first or second day of training on the race circuit that Pete had a fairly nasty accident crossing a bridge on a twisting descent. He was pretty badly cut and shaken so, yes; we needed a team nurse who happened to be my mum! She tended to Pete's injuries and he was fighting fit by the time the first race came along.

I don't remember Pete's race results at that particular event, but I know he placed much higher in his class than I did in mine and I do remember that despite me fast-track training programme he was still significantly faster than me. I was determined to catch him, and I think I probably achieved that two years later at the 1984 Winter Paralympic Games in Innsbruck, Austria.

In the meantime, our paths crossed on the running track as he joined me on the British Paralympic Athletics Team. We attended many training weekends together. It's a fact that blind runners struggle to get guides who are fast enough to run with them at international competition level. The same was true for Pete and he sometimes showed up at training weekends guide-less. I was able to stand in as I could see enough to run with him on the track as long as there weren't too many other athletes in our way!

It was a real case of 'the blind leading the blind'. Despite Pete still being quicker on skis than me, I had the upper hand in running shoes, so was able to train and even race with him. I've guided a number of blind athletes in my time including the multi-world-record-holding legend that is the late Bob Matthews MBE who was the first totally blind man to run sub 2 minutes for 800 metres.

But Pete was the only runner I knew of who preferred to go on the right side of his guide – this may have changed in later years. This meant I found it quite hard to steer him around the bends of an athletics track. With your runner on your left side the guide can lean slightly on his or her shoulder to indicate the bend of the track. With the runner on the right one has to work harder to use the guide rope/hand to steer. On the other hand, Pete was so nimble in his movements and so trusting that this made up for the unorthodox choice to run on the outside.

James became part of the group containing many of Peter's friends from his school days with whom he had remained firm friends. He recalls a training trip in the early 1980s, where a group of them, blind and partially sighted, lived together:

Around this time, between '82 and '84, we spent a week in a cabin together in Norway. We were there to train of course, and our guides would pick us up from the cabin in the mornings to take us out on the ski tracks. Overnight we were left to our own devices. I remember some of the lively debates, verging on arguments, that took place in that cabin, particularly between Ken Bodden, a blind, black, piano-tuning communist revolutionary Mancunian from Panama, and Pete, whose political views differed significantly!

As with many others who got to know Peter, it was not only beer, women and skiing that filled his life. He loved music, and played the piano extremely well; once again, self-taught and done so that he could test how well he had tuned pianos. He was extremely good at what he did and was called to the Royal Albert Hall in order to tune the grand pianos prior to large concerts.

Again, James has fond memories:

> That was also when I began to learn of the music that filled Pete's life and the lives of my fellow ski teammates. They were all wonderful musicians. They all sang in harmonies, Pete played piano whilst Ken was a superb guitarist. Beer was a significant feature of our training camps – something that couldn't happen these days – and after a few pints the songs that emerged ranged from the war-time classics, through Motown to some of the choicest rugby songs I've ever heard! At the age of 17 I'd never heard many of the words that appeared frequently in the verses of those musical masterpieces!
>
> I don't remember the year, probably '85, we took ourselves on a training camp to Austria. We didn't have any funds to pay for our Norwegian ski guides to fly over, so we had to cope without. Being the most sighted in the party (having 5% in my good eye) I led the group of five. Pete followed, then Ken, Mike and finally Jimmy (Denton) who still had a small amount of useful sight at the time. Whilst this was absolutely not ideal because we really all needed individual guides, we somehow managed to get some great training in as we just guided each other by shouting instructions back down the line: 'slight left, bad right track, steep climb, Herringbone,

long straight descent coming, brake, brake, brake, STOP'. At one point we pulled into the overtaking lane at speed to get around a group of slightly slower skiers who were, somewhat oddly, all dressed in white. They caught us again on a fast descent where we had to be cautious due to many rocks, trees and a vertical drop off the side of the track. It was at that point we discovered they were British Marines taking part in their annual championships! To say they were embarrassed to be overtaken by a bunch of blind guys is an understatement. But we all bought each other pints of Austrian beer later that evening in town and made up!

Again, the British team trained hard, yet they maintained the tradition they had started at the onset and when the work and training was done, it was time to party.

We had finished skiing for the week and decided to have a proper night out. This involved taking Ken's guitar up to Max's Bar (a place we knew well) and entertaining all and sundry with our repertoire. We created a real party scene. Max joined us at our table and all the other customers pulled up their stools too. Later in the evening when most had gone Pete and I decided we'd become the bar staff, so went behind and started serving the remaining customers as well as ourselves! I recall Pete's joy in his new role as he used the very subtle finger-dip method to know when the draught beer was nearing the top of the glasses.

Back home in the UK, Pete and I found ourselves at a Christmas party together. I don't remember the occasion specifically, but I do remember the buffet! Our girlfriends, one of whom was fully sighted and the other partially, had helped us to get our plates loaded up with food from the finger buffet. We'd returned to our table and worked our way through sandwiches, vol-au-vents, pizza and so on. The girls then went off to dance leaving us on our own. Pete was still hungry, and we headed off to the buffet ourselves; it was never going to end well.

I couldn't see what I was loading on to the plates, but I tried to describe things to Pete as well as I could. What we didn't realize was that the caterers were in the midst of clearing the savoury course and setting out the desserts. So, we ended up with a mix of the two! Smoked salmon, jelly, ice cream and crisps never tasted so good!

The early bond, initially created by James' admiration for Peter developed into a firm friendship, and the two continued to meet and train together. But more than this, there was also a competitive edge: James being partially sighted wished to be faster than Peter; Peter totally blind wanted to be the best in the world, and no one in Britain was going to be faster than him.

James remembers how both he and Peter developed throughout the years ahead:

> Pete and I worked really hard on our ski training through the late eighties and early nineties. We had similar aspirations to reach the medal-winning positions at World and Paralympic level. By then we'd recruited a very slick team of skiing guides and assistants, all Norwegian of course. Peter had gotten a new guide, a young lad who was pretty quick on his feet and managed to push Peter hard. He was fully sighted and although he never came to the ski events until some stage around 1994 or so, him and Peter were like one unit together. For someone who had been a guide it was quite fascinating to watch, and I understand that a lot of the other runners needing guides at Metro were just a tiny bit jealous. Either way, they trained together, a lot! And Peter met always in good nick. In addition to this Mike Brace had done a stunning job of fundraising and we got some great sponsorship from equipment manufacturers. This was

unheard of and how Mike managed it I really do not know. It was never published anywhere, nothing was really ever published about the para, or about disabled sport in general to be honest.

Prior to then we'd each had just one guide who also had to do most of the ski prep and testing on race day. This often meant we didn't get a full warm-up before the start. By 1990 we were able to afford to take extra guides who could help with prep and also swap places on longer races. Skiing at race pace, shouting instructions constantly with the heartrate almost at max is tough so we were able to switch to a fresh guide part way through which had the additional benefit of a psychological boost from the fresh guide. And this is when the medals really started to happen.

For a non-snow nation to pick up top results in cross-country skiing was really remarkable. Pete and I consistently beat rivals from Norway, Sweden, Finland, Russia, USA, Germany, France, Austria, Czechoslovakia, and the rest. I think Pete took his first gold at the 1990 World Championships in the US. I don't remember his result at the '92 Paralympic Games in Albertville, France but I do remember our team performance in the relay.

Ordinarily most cross-country races at the time were more of a time-trial against the clock. Each skier and guide started separately at half or one-minute intervals. By contrast the relay is a mass start. So, here's yet another wonderful sight to behold. Every nation placed their quickest skiers on the first leg of the relay where we would line up side-by-side on the start line. This requires a fair bit of space with a track cut in the snow for each pair of skiers. But soon after the start the number of tracks begins to reduce, and within a couple of hundred meters we're funnelled into just two tracks. So, the start is critical and pretty aggressive.

As many as twenty countries would be represented, meaning that, with guides, there were forty athletes battling one another for position. I always led out for GB and in 1992 was guided by my wonderful friend, Dag Olimbe. We had developed a fairly unique technique for the relay start. We went out super hard shouting and screaming as we went in our attempt to distract others and interrupt communications between them and their guides. On this occasion the technique worked brilliantly and, somehow, we emerged onto the narrowing tracks in third position. The adrenaline seemed to carry us through.

I was ahead of almost everyone who would normally beat me, with only two ahead to catch. Coming down hill into a tunnel we were gaining on France, the home team. Dag was yelling his head off again, more to encourage me than to distract the French. We were right on their shoulder when my rival slipped out of the track with one ski on the bend in the tunnel, so Dag and I dug really deep and managed to overtake.

The excitement as we got into the stadium to hand over to Pete was incredible. Great Britain holding second place in the Winter Paralympic cross-country relay! Thinking about this as I write gives me goose-bumps! Pete who was in the form of his life took over from me and gave it everything. I was totally exhausted, and I think Dag was too. But we bellowed our support to Pete as we tapped him off the start line. The rules of the relay stated that each team had to have two totally blind skiers amongst its numbers. All countries placed their fastest skier first, often this was also the most sighted team member too which was important for the mass start. Next the strategy would be to send off your best totally blind skier. So, Pete was up against rivals from his own class as he set off and he managed to hold position through his lap; he may even have made ground on the leading skier but didn't get past. Sadly, we'd dropped back out of the medals by the time our fourth skier finished but, as a team, we could not believe our success and as individual athletes, Pete and I were unbelievably proud of our individual performances that day.

Whilst training Peter liked nothing better than to try and break his guide, something that Dag recalls with fondness:

We were training in Beitostølen I remember; there is little downhill, and we chose an area that was formed in a flat figure of eight so I could allow Pete to go ahead to press himself. I remember there were a few people there when we started and whilst I was preparing the skis Peter was getting himself warm. I gave him his skis and before I had even had a chance to take off my jacket Pete was off down the tracks like a bat out of hell.

Worried that he would collide with other users of the track Dag striped down to his training clothing, put on his skis and then set out after Peter.

He recollects:

He was really moving, and I was not even warmed up, it was well below freezing and it did not take long before my muscles stiffened. I was only a short distance behind Pete at that time and shouted to someone that I knew at the side of the track to take over and make sure Peter never collided with anyone or anything or hurt himself. My lungs were bursting, not because I couldn't keep up, but because I had gone from a resting state to one of flat out exertion and was suffering badly from lactic build up just about everywhere.

I ended up crossing the tracks and meeting Peter along with a rather exhausted 'guide' as he rounded the figure eight and was able to take over properly from there. Pete on the other hand never let me live that down and made it his mission to try to break all of his guides, no matter what; he found it fun in his own way.

Like many other he was surprised at Peter's total commitment and enjoyed his time guiding. Peter and Dag formed a strong bond and friendship despite the age difference and both Dag and Trond became Peter's first choice of guide when they were available to do so. Trond stopped guiding Peter after the World Championships in New Hampshire in 1990 but they remained strong and firm friends.

Peter now had everything he needed: guides in the UK to aid and assist his general training, the support of a renowned athletics coach, a profession that allowed him to train on snow when it arrived, and a couple of very good skiing guides who were at elite level in their own right.

In a further attempt to get even more training into his repertoire, and to not be totally dependent on guides and treadmills, Peter joined the Metro cycling club and was paired with a woman named Katie. Once again Peter had a new string to his bow. His decision to join was calculated: although it may not be the same conditioning as achieved when running, training on the bike was most definitely much better than training on the treadmill. The cycling strengthened his thighs, which in turn assisted his running and skiing. For Peter, nothing was ever done without a purpose, and nothing that was done would be detrimental to his chances of becoming the best he could be, the best in the world.

In the autumn of 1990 Peter also enlisted the help of a guy named Lyder Sunde, who was based further north in Norway in a village called Spillum in Namdalen, Northern Trøndelag. Lyder was also a very competent skier and had just stopped competing for himself. His sister Torunn had been involved with the Norwegian team and had met Peter, so she acted as a middleman at first. He recalls the first meeting:

I thought it was really exciting and after the first meeting with Peter became fascinated by the person and not just the athlete and felt that I had something to contribute to his training. He also became a really good friend and came to visit us for training and just to be social a few times a year. When he died, I can honestly say there are few people I have missed as much as I do Peter.

Peter and his two guides, Dag and Lyder, became a formidable group, seen at all major competitions, all of them with extreme determination, none of them liking to come second.

They worked to Peter's strengths. He had not learned to 'skate' on skis as some of his Norwegian competitors who had previously been sighted had and that put him at a disadvantage. The freestyle or skating technique is much faster than using the classic style of almost running on skis.

Lyder recalls:

> Peter was amazing at using his poles, either singularly as
> if he was running, but even more so when he used them
> double. He managed to generate a massive amount of
> power through his upper body and through his legs and,
> to be fair, it was not uncommon for this to be so explosive
> it caught Dag and myself out, and we ourselves needed
> to step up a gear in order to guide him.

The fact that both Peters guides were Norwegian did not detract
from the fact that they too wanted Peter to be the best he could be, to
be the best, and if that meant they had to beat their own countrymen
to do so, then so be it.

3

A Force to Be Reckoned With

His successes of the 1984 winter season along with his new view on training, plus the benefits he had gained from having regular winter training guides, gave Peter even greater motivation. He continued cycling and weight training as well as running and was selected for the 1984 summer games in New York. As will be explained a little later this did not go as planned and there was a stage when he doubted himself and whether he was indeed cut out to be a challenger on the world stage after all.

He spent more time on the cycle than before, and more time on the treadmill. Derek was now nearing his best and the summer season saw speed and track work, something that really was not Peter's forte. The winter saw gruelling cross-country competitions and although Peter took part in some, he was always conscious that he would not hold back Derek who was faster than him and who was pursuing his own career. After all, Derek was helping him, and he was in no position to make demands.

Gerry had now moved to Colchester, which was some 35–40 miles from where Peter lived, and this made training even more difficult. Gerry was extremely conscious of this and tried his best to fit in a couple of days a week or a long run at the weekend. I personally met Gerry only once or twice, but at that time felt as though I was under the microscope as the 'trainee guide' and we never really gained any connection. This was a real shame as I feel in hindsight that Pete would have benefitted greatly from having us both in his corner.

There were no major events happening in 1985 so Peter spent the year conditioning himself and spending as much time as he could on snow in Norway. He had been married for around 3 years by this time to Kathy, yet his training came first as far as he was concerned and Kathy to her credit stood firmly beside him, accompanying him to Norway and on his other travels.

In 1986, only 2 years after winning Olympic bronze in Calgary, and really attacking his training and competitive life, Peter was back in the tracks and competing in the World championships held in Sälen, Sweden. He competed in three events, the 10-kilometre classic race, the 20-kilometre classic, and the biathlon, which at that time was not a recognized Olympic event and would not become so for another 6 or more years.

Once again, Peter stood on the podium winning a bronze medal in the 10-kilometre classic race. He raced well but once more was beaten by his two arch-rivals, Terje and Magne. Peter was pleased with the race; however, the other events did not go as planned and he was not placed in medal winning positions.

This time Peter's motivation was not spurred by his success, but by his failure to win anything higher than bronze. On a positive note, Peter had arrived on the international scene and the other competitors, who once saw an overweight and out of shape Englishman, now saw a motivated and well-trained competitor whom they all needed to take seriously.

The following year the European Championships were on the calendar. Peter sat down with John and planned a training strategy worthy of the world's elite (which in essence he was now a part of).

Ski training in the winter months went without any major hiccups other than the odd cold and virus but skiing alone was not enough and the running he did play a major role in his fitness. Sadly, this was still not at the level Peter wanted. The training was done to the best of his abilities and the time that he had available, but still proved to be inadequate. Peter was now faster than Gerry other than on long runs and this in turn meant that he sometimes missed vital interval and speed endurance sessions, both of which are of paramount importance in the lives of middle- and long-distance athletes, regardless of whether they ski, run or cycle.

However, being who he was, Peter would not make demands on people. He knew that without the time others put aside for him he would not be able to run at all on the roads and would be confined to the treadmill. Despite the treadmill being better than nothing, it is far removed from the real world of running, where terrain adds a great deal to the training for free.

Upon arriving at the European Championships, Peter was prepared as best as he could be. Dag and Trond were on hand to guide as usual and had a great way of pressing Peter to dig slightly deeper than he wanted.

Again Peter competed in the same events, 10-kilometre classic, 20-kilometre classic and biathlon; again he was beaten by the two Norwegians, Terje and Magne, but this time, he won bronze in all three events, ensuring him a position in British athletics history as the highest awarded winter athlete Britain had produced at that time. Again, Peter was inspired, he was motivated again by both the disappointment and also the success of standing on the podium for all three of his chosen events.

He was now an international veteran at age 31, having competed in five major international events and winning five medals in total. Sadly, the colour of these medals was the same, bronze, and Peter was determined that the colour needed to change to something 'brighter' as he put it.

The winter of 1988, however, saw a bit of a form dip for Peter as he competed in the World Championships in Trento, Austria. Although he had trained as best as he could he was not in the condition he needed to be in for several reasons and wasn't placed in any of the events he had entered.

A despondent and disappointed Peter returned to the UK afterwards and knew that he needed to make some changes in order to lift himself to the level he needed to be at. Peter's focus was once more on his conditioning and on analysing what he needed in order to compete with the Norwegians who were a constant thorn in his side. He had yet to find a weakness in them; they appeared invincible, but he was determined.

Around this time, he also realized that he was in desperate need of more consistent running guides. He was not well known in the area and, although he had a network of friends, there were few runners in the area that were fast enough to match him. Of those that were, most had aspirations to pursue a successful career on the track themselves, and Peter was not a selfish man expecting people to put him first.

He continued to train with Gerry sporadically and with Derek when the opportunity arose, but conducted much of his running on the treadmill, and his other training on the tandem cycle behind Katie.

Cycling was safe and it did not matter if Katie was not fast or strong enough to match him; her job on the cycle was to steer and stop the tandem cycle . Pete could push himself as hard as he wanted whilst cycling and although It was far from optimal, it was the best he could do at that time.

In the winter of 1989 Peter was once again back in the ski tracks with Dag and Trond by his side. He had again trained as best as was possible given the restraints he had and the limited amount of time he had on snow.

The lack of snow time meant he was not able to focus on the ski technique, which was an area where he knew he could improve. All his training trips away were self-funded and there was no public sponsorship or funding available despite Mike Brace doing what he could.

This was a problem throughout the late 1980s and 90s. Britain excelled on the track and field athletics scene, with both Peter Elliot and Steve Cram joining the likes of Steve Ovett, Sebastian Coe and decathletes Daley Thompson and Eugene Gilkes, to name but a few.

The British medias' focus was on these people and the campaign to have Sebastian Coe reinstated into the British Olympic team in order for him to attempt to win a triple 1500 metre Olympic title in 1988 was I remember huge, taking up pages of the tabloids for weeks. As a huge Coe fan, I can remember ringing up quite a telephone bill on the voting line set up by one of the tabloids. I was horrified that he would not be going.

But, looking back on this experience a couple of years later, it seemed incredible that when disabled athletes, whom the general British public had never even heard of, were winning medals, that they never received a single line to actually acknowledge their great achievements.

Owing to his lack of running practice Peter did not feel that he was in the best physical condition to take part in all three of the events he liked the best. He had not done the work, he was missing pure speed and speed endurance, and so he settled for the longest race that he could, the 20-kilometre classic event.

He skied well and was strong throughout, but the elements he had missed throughout training caught up with him. Once more he was beaten, but this time only by one of his Norwegian rivals, Terje, forcing Magne Lunde into third place.

His medal had become a different colour, had become brighter, and he was now completely sure that he would be able to match the other skiers all the way to the line, providing he managed to complete the training he needed, when he needed it and in the way it needed to be done.

But racing aside, the fun side of Peter and the British team in general remained the same. It was certainly this that attracted the Norwegian guides and made them feel so welcome. Dag recalls an incident after Peter had won the silver medal in 1989.

> We were preparing for the race, training, eating and resting. Peter decided that too much seriousness was as damaging as too much partying, so we decided to go for a drink one evening, a few days before we were due to race. We dressed up a bit smart leaving thick boots and ski

clothes behind and were stupid enough to go out in flat dress shoes.

Things kind of took off as was often the case with the boys when they went for a drink and it must have quite late when we decided to go back to the hotel. On the way back we ran down a rather steep hill, in minus degrees, with packed snow on the floor, and in flat shoes. It was really slippery, and we were worried about falling and injuring ourselves, but we survived and thought nothing more of it.

The evening was over, and they retired to rest ready to start final preparation the next day. Dag remembers:

I woke the next morning but was not hungover or feeling worse for wear after a few beers the night before, but when I got out of bed I could barely move. My calves and the muscles running next to my shins were completely cramped and stiff, it was awful and can only have been caused by running downhill in bad footwear.

I collected Pete for breakfast and saw he was limping and struggling the same as I, but neither of us said anything to the other. There was no way either he or I were going to admit to something being wrong, so we just got on with it. There was a sense of relief after the race when we both spoke of it.

Having several guides available to run with at home was a blessing, it provided a back-up should one become injured or ill, but it was not the best arrangement and Peter being the man he was, informed Derek and Gerry that he would be looking for others. The search started in mid spring of 1989 after the winter season had finished, and a new episode for both Peter and I began.

4

A New Era

THE YELLOW ADVERTISER: ONE PERSON REPLIES

Peter ran with his guides, Gerry Madden and Derek Coates, until around the late spring of 1989, when Peter had decided he needed to have more consistency in his training and that he would look for others. By this time Peter, aged almost 33, was well versed in aspects of training and knew that if he was going to be able to compete successfully in the Para Nordic Skiing World Championships in New Hampshire in the early part of 1990, then he needed to find another guide, or guides, and quickly.

Based on the fact that at the time Peter was not well known in the area, and that the internet was still only a pipe dream, Peter and his family contacted the local free newspapers in the hope that someone somewhere could either help directly or knew someone who could.

And so, began my history with Peter. I lived along the A13 in Dagenham, the main road from Central London through to the Thames Estuary in Southend, some 30 miles or so away. For some reason none of the local free newspapers were delivered to our home. Not that that ever really bothered us, but in this particular instance, it would have most likely meant that Pete and I would never have met. It was in essence a real sliding-doors moment for us. At the time I had started studying for my A levels at school. A friend of mine, Rob Biddiss, lived in a much quieter road and got the newspapers through his door. One day he brought the article about Peter into school and during a free study period put it in front of me. He never said much other than, 'Thought this might interest you Dave'. He was certainly right.

However, I was unsure as to how to approach this. I had worked voluntarily with disabled people as part of a sixth-form school class. I and the others who had enrolled in this class had enjoyed these encounters so much that we continued to meet with them. But I had never any real contact with the blind or visually impaired. Sure, I had seen the piano tuners at school (one of whom might well have been Pete when I think about it), but most of these had dogs to help, and the article gave absolutely no idea as to how to contact the guy in the picture. This guy was 33, looked extremely fit, and was stating in the newspaper article that his current guides were no longer fast enough, and he was looking for new ones.

I spoke again with Rob briefly over the next couple of days and it was he who suggested the really simple idea of getting in touch with the journalist who had written the article in the first place. So, I did. But it was around June at this time, right in the middle of exams, and right at the start of the holiday season. Sods Law being what it is, the journalist was on holiday. I thought that would be the end but tried again the week after and managed to get through to him. For some reason he sounded genuinely shocked that someone had answered the article, almost as if it was an unexpected result that such a long shot would pay off.

He gave me a telephone number and the only thing I could do was man up, pick up the phone and try to call someone I knew nothing about, had never seen and had never heard of, but with whom I hoped to gain some mutual benefit from training alongside.

At this time, I was a budding and aspiring club and county level middle-distance runner. I was a little disappointed that my progress was slower than I wanted, and a little disillusioned that I was training in a group that was possibly more directed at those wishing to run the longer distances. The club, Newham and Essex Beagles, was well known and an historical club in the world of British Athletics; it boasted some fine names: Olympians Daley Thompson, Eugene Gilkes and Colin Reitz, and later the likes of Matthew Yates who reached stardom in the 1990 Commonwealth Games by coming an unexpected third in the 800 metres, beating the likes of Sebastian Coe in the process. Matthew went on to win the indoor European Championships a few years later and represented his country until around 1998.

But, despite the club's history and its relatively near location, I was struggling to train. Track days were fine, but I pretty much ran alone otherwise, and sometimes my training was too sporadic. I never had the determination to go out in all weathers and get the job done. My hope was that for a couple of days a week this guy, Peter Young, and I could both get something we needed out of a running partnership.

So, I picked up the phone, and with my heart thumping in my chest and my speech of introduction planned, I made the call. There was no answer. Nothing, it just rang off. In the days before the mobile telephone there was nothing else, I could do. People did not have 24 hours a day availability and were certainly not continually connected through the world of social media as they are today.

I tried calling again over the next few days, but still there was no reply, and in the end, I started wondering if it was worth the effort to keep calling someone when there was no answer. Maybe I had the wrong number? I called the journalist again; he confirmed the number, took mine and said he too would try. I was the only one who had responded to the article and, well, it would be a shame if nothing came of it, right? After nearly 3 weeks I had almost given up. I had tried to call over a dozen times in those weeks, yet the same thing each time: no answer. I thought it best just to drop it.

Then quite late one Wednesday evening the telephone rang its monotonic tone through our front room. My dad answered, I remember, and it sounded kind of serious; this was not so unusual in essence. Despite my commitment to running not being what it should be, I was still a sub two minute 800-metre club runner and every now and then got called for British League matches when there was a shortage of people available. I naturally thought that I was going to be asked to compete, at a level I was far from comfortable with.

My dad handed me the phone, the voice was not that of the team manager, Tony, but a voice I had never heard before. It sounded cheerful and good-humoured, yet serious enough to demand respect. It was the guy from the paper, the guy I had been trying to contact, and the guy I had almost given up on. He explained that he had not long been back from holiday and that the journalist had been in touch. He started asking a few questions: my age, what I did, how often I ran, what level I was at, etc.

Then out of the blue he said, 'Well, righto then mate, we better get a run in, eh'. I had obviously given him the right answers. We arranged to meet the following evening. I was working part-time at Texas Homecare as one of 'Toms Helpers' at the time and did not finish until 8 pm. Peter provided me with his address and gave me directions from where I worked, and we hung up.

I woke the next morning with mixed emotions: I was excited, yet at the same time scared and nervous. I couldn't work out why at first. It was Thursday, there was nothing really different: school, homework, part-time work, then a run. It was only then I realized what I had committed to. I was going to meet and run with someone without any prior knowledge of what was expected of me. I didn't even know just how blind Peter was. Could he see light and dark? Could he see anything at all?

How the hell did you guide? I mean by this time it was getting on for late August, later even, it was dark at 8 pm, and I was going to road run with this guy who couldn't see, and me with no experience. The thought was quite daunting, the feeling bordering on uncomfortable, and I could feel my nerves forming a knotted ball deep in the pit of my stomach. Strangely enough though, I never once felt like making excuses and backing out. I had said I was going to go, so I was going to go. Worst case scenario was that I would be too slow, or he would be too slow, and that would be that.

I finished work and my Dad was waiting in the car. I was not yet driving myself and didn't want to leave it too late to get to the appointment. We followed Peter's instructions to the letter, got to the address and when Peter answered the door there was an immediate connection. It was electrifying and totally spontaneous, even before a word had been spoken, even before he had shaken my hand. It's strange but sometimes you just meet someone, and the connection is there instantly. The connection we had, this unexplained chemistry, was something that is rarely experienced, and I believe it was this connection that made us work so well together as a team. Not just in running circles, but in other areas generally. It was also this connection that caused the only argument we had in our time together. I believe to this day, that in many cases, when there are no visual stimuli then the feelings one gets are real and ones to be trusted. I saw Pete obviously, but he never saw me. Yet not once was there any sound of doubt in his voice. Of course, this could have been bravado, a front to put me at ease, but to this day I do not think so.

I for my part was a nervous wreck at this first meeting. I mean the guy was an international, well trained, Olympian, more than that an Olympic medallist, and he had advertised for a new guide giving the reason for doing so that those he was running with were no longer fast enough to keep up with him. Here was I, a 17-year-old boy weighing in at around 9 stone with a decent 800 metres time, who was struggling to get out and train on my own, hoping with everything I had that I would be good enough for him, and not hold him back.

I expected to just go for a short run, to see how it all worked. I had worked with disabled people previously but had no experience with blind people. Guiding in Peter's case was done verbally and with him and me holding each end of a short piece of looped knotted rope. Pete ran on my right and told me it was important I ran naturally. He was the one who would adjust to my style and not the other way around. I was somewhat taller than him and was surprised how easily he matched my stride length. After about five strides he was in sync; it was almost as though we were running a three-legged race, no chopping and changing, just free natural running.

Prior to this, I, like many others, saw a disabled person as someone in a wheelchair. My eyes were firmly opened during that first run. We ended up running 6 miles. I guess I pushed the pace a little because I did not want to hold him back. To my surprise Peter was in fantastic running condition. He gave me small pointers of what to tell him, how and when, but other than that left it pretty much down to me to decide how I was going to guide. This I found out at a later stage was not standard practice between guide and athlete, and I think that the immediate connection I had experienced with him made it even better, especially as we got used to each other's running habits. Today there are "Guide Training courses" available, but for me I find it extremely difficult to see how this works. Everyone is different and although there are standard rules of thumb in guiding, each runner has preferences. Peter liked to run on a short length of rope, other prefer longer. He preferred to run on the guides right side, others prefer the left. The bond between guide and athlete is founded on trust. He trusted me implicitly and completely from the first run. It was great. I was happy, he was happy, and we arranged to run the following day.

We had not discussed anything about how often or when we would run next, but to be honest I really don't think it mattered. After that first run, I was hooked. Pete was a nice guy, knew what he wanted but was patient. He understood that I too was hoping for a running career ahead of me, something in which he played a massive part with regard to helping me to sort out my training. He was cautious with his advice at first, but after about 3 months I found out something very important about Peter Young, and that was if he had something to say, he was going to say it; and if it was not what you wanted to hear you had two choices: try and forget it had been said, or deal with it. In my case he only ever had my best interests at heart. Sometimes I listened to him and wished I had not; other times I never listened to him and wished that I had. But those stories do not belong here and are mine! By the end of the evening, we had decided to run again the next day.

The next day saw the British weather at its absolute best. Hammering down with rain, it was coming down so hard it bounced off the pavements. I met Peter at his bus, and we walked home to my parents' house. I was still living at home at that stage and studying for my A levels. By the time we had walked the few hundred metres we were already drowned. Peter introduced himself to my mother, who had made a point of making sure there was nothing he could fall over, and the dog came running like a whirlwind. A new playmate!

The next thing that happened is something I will never forget. The dog, a Jack Russel terrier, was a boisterous little dog. She was genuinely happy all the time, and loved people, especially if she had never met them before. She barked a bit but when Peter crouched down to say hello, she stopped completely still in a kind of stunned way. The only explanation that comes to mind is that Peter's eyes were glass (something I never discovered for about another 4 years) and gave absolutely no indication of what he was thinking or feeling. So, the dog stopped, sniffed, accepted, and then walked back to her basket and kept out of the way. He had a way with animals that was apparent on numerous occasions. He even taught my pet cockatiel to say some phrases, which would most definitely not have been accepted in church, and most certainly do not belong here.

So, running we went. I had no real planned route and sort of made it up as we went along. We were completely soaked in a matter of minutes. Over the course of the hour we were out I learned probably one of the most important lessons ever when guiding someone who is visually impaired. Concentrate and look where you are going! We were running along the pavement and I got distracted by something, although I cannot now remember what it was. As we came to a curb I slowed, thinking we might have to stop in order to let the traffic pass. Seeing a gap, and forgetting Peter was there, I ran dragging him with me and he crashed into a concrete bollard marking the crossing point on the road. It hit him hard just below the knee, but he said nothing.

After we had crossed, I looked down and saw an abrasion on Peter's leg, made to look worse as the rain mixed with the blood. Pete brushed it off, saying there was nothing to be done about it. We finished our run, changed and had a cuppa. Dad and I then drove him back to his parents' house. Dad waited outside for a while as he knew I was going to go in. My dad was great like that, and for the first few months until I passed my test it made things easier for Peter and me to train without having to rely on late night runs or public transport.

The area where Peter's parents lived was about 15 minutes' drive from where I lived. I had never been around this way before and the road names meant absolutely nothing to me. But Pete was like a living A to Z road map. He told us what to look for, what the road names were, what colour cars to park by. I swore to myself that this guy was conning me and that he really could see.

Nervously I went into the house with Peter to find his mum and dad in the kitchen. Dinner was cooking and Peter introduced me as Dave, the new guide. His mum and dad looked a little shocked; this tall skinny kid walking in with their son – there was quite an age gap between us. None the less they said hello. Joan and Sid were fantastic people, and both were obviously immensely proud of Peter and well they should be. They were in their early 60s at that time and his mum did love her Senior Service cigarettes. They were both typical East Enders, and I think had lived in the house for pretty much most of their lives. I found out that Peter had two brothers, David and Paul, one older, one younger, plus a mass of nieces and nephews. Peter's family were close knit, and they spoke about absolutely everything, loudly and not worrying about who heard what.

In good old East End fashion, the kettle was never far from boiling and Joan had put it on as soon as she heard the car pull up. The radio was on and I was chatting to Sid; he wanted to know the usual stuff: where I lived, what I did, was I fast enough for Pete, and would I be

50

willing to commit to guiding. After all, Pete did have a World Championship to race in the second week of January, only 12 or 14 weeks away. Besides, Peter had already told his team management and his parents that he would drop out if he was not in good enough shape to compete at the level he wanted. One thing I found out at an early stage was that Peter was incredibly dedicated to what he did, as are all who compete at top level sport.

On the opposite side of the table Peter sat chatting to his mum; I only picked up snippets of the conversation at first, but after Sid went to watch the racing on the TV, I followed it a little more. Joan was also just asking Peter the usual sort of questions: She wanted to know if I was doing alright, and whether I could be trained to be the guide that Peter wanted me to be. Peter raised his eyebrow, and speaking out of the corner of his mouth, told Joan about the incident that had happened a little earlier with the concrete bollard. She did her motherly tut and Peter continued, telling his mum about me and declaring, 'the dozy cunt had not even seen the bloody thing', and finishing with 'and the bastards call me fucking blind'.

Joan chuckled and seeing my embarrassment and discomfort told me not to mind him, and that if he had been upset with me, he would have told me there and then. I found out a couple of months later that Peter was not easily offended and was quite happy to make a mockery of himself and his disability, if you could call it that.

I learned from an early stage that Peter Young was as honest as they come and expected nothing less in return. If you really didn't want an answer to a question, then you shouldn't ask. If you were asked a question, he would read you like a book, and knew if you were lying. It was quite strange in some ways, but after no more than 3 weeks we got to understand each other and developed a guiding pattern from which we both gained a massive amount. I helped Peter run faster, Peter taught me to use senses that I took for granted and got me out training properly. In regard to training, I did my own track work Mondays and Wednesdays, and initially ran with him on

Tuesdays and Thursdays. In those days, Peter decided what he needed in regard to training; my job, was to be there and help him get it done. On the days we never ran, we spoke on the phone and the bond between us developed incredibly quickly.

After about a month or so Peter decided he needed more stamina and asked if I had any more time to spare. He said he could try contacting an old guide if not and that there was no obligation. I had noticed an increase in my own fitness during the weeks I had been running with Peter and could only put this down to the fact that I was training consistently. I told Pete that other than my own track days and any race days I might have; I would be able to run as often as he wanted. From that moment we increased from 2 days a week to 4, meaning I was running 6 days with 1-day rest, Peter 4 days running, 2 days cycling and then 1-day rest. The increase in conditioning and running form was noticeable within a very short space of time.

By this time, I had finished my A levels and had started working for Barking and Dagenham Council on their career trainee scheme; more importantly, I had passed my driving test. The offices were literally no more than a 5-minute drive from Peter's home, and it took even less time to walk, so going training was made even easier. Leaving work at a quarter to five we were on the road by five as a rule. We finished sometime between six and half past, and after a cuppa I was always home before seven in the evening. It played havoc with the evening meal, and as often as not I ate alone, but mum was great, and always made sure she had put food to one side for me. The negative thing about running as much as I did was my appetite. Pete had made it clear: if you are hungry, eat what you need, eat everything. So, seeing that this worked, I did.

One evening Peter had decided he needed some track intervals to test himself as to where he was In regard to fitness. This would have been early October 1989. So, after work we drove to the Ilford athletic track, warmed up and got down to business. I don't remember the session we ran, but it was the first time Peter and I had run on anything other than grass or the road, so I was really unsure as to what to expect. I had the advantage; the track was my domain. I was predominantly a track athlete. I knew the track, was at home on the track. What made it easier for me was that Pete ran on my right side. Meaning that I held the inside and there was little to no risk of me hitting the curb. It meant that Peter would be running central in the lane.

Here, I had a real eye-opening experience. I was slight, standing around 6 feet tall and weighing not more than 9 stone in training gear. Peter was a little shorter than me, more heavily muscled, and generally a powerhouse. My biggest concern was that I would not be physically strong enough to keep Pete where he needed to be whilst running at speed. Through the first session, I found that Peter, despite his strength, was not as fast as me and this gave me a great advantage. It meant that I was running a fair bit slower than I needed, making me and ultimately him stable on the track. I naturally leaned into the bends as I did whilst training by myself. He followed naturally, meaning we ran the bends extremely tightly, making for good track running.

We finished training, warmed down and I drove Peter home. The house was in darkness, meaning that Peter's wife was not home. His wife Kathy was also visually impaired but did have some sight, so the lights would have been on. I followed Pete to the door, thanked him for the training and he went inside. He mentioned that it felt cold and that he needed to put the heaters on if winter was going to come so early. I drove home, proud of myself, thinking that I had found a vocation, that guiding was mine and mine alone. I felt that I was making an important contribution to Peter's training and to his competitive chances in the forthcoming World Championships just the other side of the New Year.

I had not been in the door more than a few minutes when the phone rang. Kathy had come home from work and when turning on the lights had found that the house had been burgled. They had broken in through the back-patio door after climbing over the garden fence. Peter's neighbours were elderly and hard of hearing, the house dark and the back garden secluded. I don't exactly recall what if anything had been taken. Peter was rightly enough fuming; Kathy more shocked that someone had been in and rifled through their stuff, clothes and personal items. The police were called, and naturally asked if there had been anything strange or anyone new in the house of late. The answer to this was a resounding yes: Peter had a new guide. The guide was a young lad of 17, short hair, leather jacket. It was obvious wasn't it? Luckily Peter did have his head screwed on for the most part and put this theory to rest immediately telling the police we had been training and that I had dropped him home. I dread to think what might have happened had I not trained with Peter that day. Even more relevant was the fact that usually I went into the house with Peter after we had trained, but this particular day I was running late for something and needed to get home in order to get ready.

The scary part of this is the unknown: were the person or persons in the house when Peter opened the door. If they were, would I have seen them had I gone in? And what would their reaction have been? More to the point, what would Peter's reaction and mine have been, we were both still adrenaline charged from training, and the only way past would have been by the side of the house where I had parked the car. It could have gotten physical. Not something that bears thinking of right now. Luckily in this instance no one got hurt, but I did feel that there was a slight atmosphere between Peter and me for a little while after. His suspicion was obviously justified, and Peter being Peter he asked the question straight out. Had I had anything to do with it? The answer was an obvious no. Peter accepted this and we moved on.

It was not more than a couple of weeks later when Peter called me at work, something that he never did. I was a little concerned, but it turned out the BBC had gotten wind of Peter competing in the World Para Nordic Skiing Championships in New Hampshire the following January, and they wondered if we might be willing take part in some filming for their programme *Sport on Friday*.

At this stage Peter was having a hard time finding sponsorship to assist him. He was self-employed, so if he did not work, he did not get paid. The Championships were over a 10-day period and like always Peter wanted to get in a week extra on the snow. His biggest competitors were the Norwegians who had much more opportunity to practise on snow. In addition, the Norwegian competitors had previously been partially sighted and classified as, at worse, class B2, and had therefore learned their cross-country classic technique by seeing it, unlike Peter, who was and had always been totally blind, and had to learn from description and sensation.

It is important here to explain the way the visually impaired are classified into competitive classes. It is not easy to understand and took me many years to get a hold of it.

The visually impaired are split into three classes, B1, B2, and B3. B1 is for those that are the most impaired, and B3 for those who see best of all. That said, those in B3 still have extremely poor vision but there is generally no need for a guide runner.

A B1 athlete is one who has little or no sight and cannot see shapes or movement of, for example, a hand, if it is waved in front of them. They may be able to see light and dark.

A B2 classification is for those who have 2/60 vision or an acuity less than 5 degrees. In layman's terms this means that what a normally sighted person would see at 60 feet, they would see at 2 feet. The acuity is the field of vision, meaning they have less than 5 degrees field of sight.

B3 classification is given to those with 6/60 vision. Again, in layman's terms this means what a normally sighted person will see at 60ft, a B3 Athlete will see at 6. Their field of vision or acuity is less than 20 degrees.

This is hard to imagine for all normally sighted persons, but most of us have played blind man's bluff, trying to find other people while blindfolded. Now imagine trying to ski and focus on someone telling you what do while not being able to see.

People began to wake up to the possibility of screening serious sport competitions for the disabled. There had been TV coverage of the Summer Paralympics for a while, but people like Mike Brace and others working with the British Blind Sports Association now had a real weapon with which to make a breakthrough. They had a real British patriot, who was not only competing, but who was also a potential medallist in the Championships. His name was Peter Young, *my* Peter Young. This was not prime-time TV; it went out at around 2 pm on a Friday afternoon, but the BBC snapped it up. Peter and I agreed to take part in the filming. That afternoon was not one that would be forgotten for a very long time by anyone involved in it.

PETER RUNS THE SHOW

The day of the filming arrived. We were due to start at midday. My bosses were great and gave me the time off work, and the parks department allowed the BBC to come in with their cars in order to film some running. The park chiefs of Hainault Forest did the same and cordoned off an area for us to use. It was like being a celebrity for the afternoon, and although we enjoyed it, we thought that we might as well include the filming of us running as part of our training; after all we were in preparation for a championship event in just about 6 weeks, and this would have been a normal running day for us.

Whilst we were waiting for everyone to arrive at Pete's house, there was a lot of discussion as to where and how we were going to film. Peter and I were local to the area and decided that Hainault Forest was the best place to start, being farthest away.

We thought we were ready to go when there was yet another knock at the door and Gerald Sinstadt, the well-known football and sports commentator, came in. He was truly a lovely man, said hi to us and decided he wanted to know a lot more about us prior to the run. He had no background information and the world of TV can be difficult without any kind of script.

56

At last we got to Hainault and we started with a few ski-related exercises. The cameras were at a distance, luckily for us, and the first set of exercises saw Pete bounding up a hill carrying ski poles. There were no microphones on. This was a godsend to be fair as Peter was not amused about the amount of time that had been wasted waiting around in the cold; it was getting into mid-November, it was cold and dull, and we had warmed up and were ready a good half an hour before they decided to film. The last thing we wanted was for either of us to pull a hamstring this close to the event. It would have been disastrous. We ended up turning our backs to the camera at one point in order to hide the grins on our faces as Peter vented his frustration. The training was meant to be extremely serious.

Then we ran a little on the grass, the same stretch over and over again. The shot had to be perfect, so Pete and I decided that we might as well run the short repetitions hard and fast. The camera men looked a little shocked as we ran pretty much full pelt along the grass, no words, and just two people running as one. We really gelled and I believe to this day we opened the eyes of those who saw us. I guess, for many, seeing two people being filmed was maybe remarkable enough; the fact that we were running in lycra running tights, which were not that common back then, and running whilst what looked like holding hands certainly turned heads.

We were to leave Hainault and make our way back to Dagenham. The idea that was once we got back to Central Park the film crew could drive next to us, get a feel for how we moved together, and try and gain an insight into how we managed to run as we did. At the time I had a temperamental old Vauxhall Chevette which decided not to start; the starter motor had got stuck. Next step was a crew member behind the wheel, with Pete and I pushing the car along the drive in and hoping that we could jump start it. This became a joke for the rest of the afternoon, but we did get our own back, and Pete then literally took the roof off later that afternoon. He really did have to get the final word in, as always.

We ran a few intervals of around 300 metres in Central Park, Dagenham. The camera crew had permission to drive next to us. Both Pete and I were a little despondent about the amount of time it took for them to decide how they wanted to film angles, directions, etc. We were high on adrenaline after both running and pushing the car so when the time came to run, we decided that we were going to really run!

We were running around a shallow right-hand bend, meaning that this time Peter was closest to the inside. The car was on the path so we had only the grass to run on; there were no obstacles to speak of but there was a 4-inch curb that could have proven problematical had we stepped off it. By this time, we had transferred the way we ran bends on the track on to the road. It was simple. I would say one single word 'tight' and move my rope arm (the right one) down to just below the hip on its normal path of travel. My arm movement would become shallower matching Pete's. He would lean in on me allowing me to steer the corner as I wanted, before it naturally straightened out and we could regain a normal stride pattern on the straight.

This particular bend was a beauty and we quite literally flew around it. We were moving well, fluidly and easily, the car accelerating next to us as a cameraman hung out of the window. He looked a little shell-shocked if the truth be known. We finished the run, eased off and turned around, our breathing hard but not out of control by any means.

The car had turned, and the driver asked if we could do it again, in the opposite direction. Obviously, this was not a problem; we were used to running intervals after a brief recovery anyway. Let's do it! The crew looked at us a little disbelievingly as we started the next run. This time the bend was a normal left-handed bend, exactly as on the track. As we started to run the bend Pete gave two small little tugs on the rope. To those who did not know, this was insignificant and would mean nothing. To Pete and me it meant one thing: FASTER. So, we opened the stride and away we went. I am not sure, but I believe there was some kind of expletive that escaped the cameraman's lips as the car had to accelerate in order to keep the shot. As we eased off, Pete spoke to me out the corner of his mouth, smiled and said, 'That fucked em, me boy'. The running was finished for the day, the training footage had been completed. Interviews were next. It was here Pete really took control, reducing crew, and narrator quite literally to tears on more than one occasion.

As part of the item on *Sport on Friday* there was a short section where we were interviewed separately by Gerald Sinstadt. It was not private, and we sat in on each other's interview, but were off camera. As we arrived back at the house, they tried to usher us straight into the living room to start the interviews. We had cooled off, were sweaty, and the weather had turned to light rain; we were wet, cold, and basically looked a mess. The first thing Pete did as we got in was ask Gerald Sinstadt to put the kettle on and make some tea. We, said Pete, needed to get ourselves presentable, and needed to shower. There were some comments from the crew about how much time it would take for us to both shower, so Pete stopped and told them that if it was a problem we would shower together, as it would save time and we only needed to freshen up a bit. The looks on some of their faces was incredible and I think they wondered if Pete and I had *that* sort of relationship. We were back in less than 10 minutes and ready to go.

They decided to interview me first and, although I don't remember all of the questions asked, I believe they were the standard type of questions. Why did I start guiding? What were my ambitions in running? Were there any problems or challenges in guiding? They were naturally interested in the part where it looked like we were holding hands. To be honest with you, it did look like we were holding hands, and as a 17-year-old boy, this was something that I was not really that comfortable with. Sure, it was fine when we were out running, but earlier bullying episodes and the homophobic views and preconceived social non-acceptance at that time did make it an issue sometimes. This came to a head a few years later whilst out on a run.

Peter sat quiet for the most part of my chat with Gerald Sinstadt but could not resist the odd heckle from the side lines, which meant that the 2- or 3-minutes footage shown took the best part of 20 minutes to record before editing. This was only the beginning. Peter was having fun; he was having a funny half hour that resulted in spilled and spluttered tea during his own turn in front of the camera. The questions he was asked were mainly about his training: how we did it, and how he knew whether he was going to be in good enough shape. It was not run-technical by any means, but they were extremely interested in first how he knew so much about training when he had no coach as such, and second how he managed to get so close to the top Norwegian skiers when he had a maximum of 42 days a year on snow.

Another thing that fascinated them was that, to Pete, his blindness was part of him. He had been blind since the age of 2, he had grown up being blind and to him it was not a disability. He could run, compete with the world's best at an extremely high level in three different events, and lived his life much the same as anyone else did. He washed clothes, he hoovered, and managed without any help to get the right bus to his place of work, wherever that should be.

They were interested in why there was little or no sponsorship available at the time for those who were not able-bodied. We had received a lot of rejection letters when we had asked for help, the responses stating that handicapped sport did not carry a high enough profile to warrant the sponsorship they offered; others said they were not interested in winter sports. But reading between the lines it was very clear. Visually impaired people were not seen as disabled enough to warrant sponsorship. Pete, being Pete, made this abundantly clear in no uncertain terms but, seeing as this was quite controversial for the late 1980s, little if any of this material made the final cut and likely ended up on the editing room floor.

Everyone had seen that Peter was a remarkable man in the way he trained and carried himself. They were curious as to what Pete saw as a challenge, the one thing he wanted to do more than anything else, and he told them — a parachute jump.

One sharp intake of breath and a few splutters later Gerald Sinstadt asked for some clarification. No one, not even I, could have been prepared for the answer that Pete gave. He said that it must be possible and with today's technology surely someone could be on the ground guiding him down, giving him warning when the ground was getting close. He had no real interest in a tandem jump; that was no fun. They questioned whether the technology was really advanced enough to do this safely. To which Pete answered quite seriously that if not he could borrow a guide dog for the day and use that on the jump instead.

Everything stopped. Gerald Sinstadt stopped the camera and composed himself. You could almost hear the cogs in his brain turning over, wondering how on earth he was going to address this. The camera restarted and the question came which was something along the lines of: 'How on earth will a guide dog help you on a parachute jump, if the technological advances of today cannot?' Peter raised his eyebrows, and with a cheeky grin, but a face deadly serious answered: 'When the lead goes slack, I will know I am going to land.' The place quite literally exploded: tea being sprayed over tabletops and equipment, crew members in hysterics, Gerald Sinstadt, being the professional he was, trying to keep his composure, and the camera still running.

When everyone had regained control, the equipment dried and tea wiped from the tables, the interview resumed. The tension was there throughout, and Gerald Sinstadt had decided he wanted this on film. He wanted people to know that a totally blind man wanted to parachute jump, alone. So, the question was asked again, and again, and again. Each time, someone in the background broke down into fits of laughter or made small woofing noises. But in the end, Peter behaved and answered: 'With technology today, I say we just go for it.'

After the programme was aired, we remained in contact with Gerald Sinstadt for several months, such was the impression Pete had made on him. We received two custom-made reflective vests from an unknown supplier; both the same apart from the white and black sign that was on the back. Peter's said, 'Pete's training team: Blind Athlete'. Mine the same but with the word 'Guide'. We wore these from early autumn right through the winter. Mine is now packed neatly into a box, as a constant reminder of that time.

THE START OF SOMETHING SPECIAL

On the back of the filming Pete realized that he was fit and that he was starting to come up to a level where he would plateau. Plateaus in training can be a pain, they can make you stagnate and also play tricks with your mind. Reaching one of these with only 5 weeks to go before you need to be at a peak is not uncommon, although I had never experienced one myself before. We went through a few runs where things seemed okay, but where when Pete put his foot on the gas there was nothing more to give. We started to get a little concerned; was he coming down with something? Had we done too much too soon and had he become over-trained? If this was the case, then there was only one thing to do and that was rest. Resting, however, for a week or more could also play tricks on the mind, and the circle would continue. We sat for a while after a post-run cup of tea and contemplated what to do. A race! We had trained hard; we had trained fully focused on the Worlds in January; we had lost a little of the fun that made running so enjoyable for us both. We both were of the opinion that when it was no longer fun then it was time to stop. This is a mantra I live by to this day in regard to running and training in general.

The experience was new: a new guide coming on board only 3 months or so before a championship event. A race would give us a new perspective. A race would force us to raise the game and show us if indeed we had gotten things dreadfully wrong just before the Championships. We started looking around.

There was a road race starting off a handicap about a week later just outside of Hainault; the closing date was gone but they accepted entries on the day. We knew the area – it was not far from where we trained on a Sunday – so we decided to have a go at it. It was much shorter than Peter wanted, not being more than 5 kilometres. Peter would be competing in the 5 kilometres in the World Championships but held no real hope for it. He was a long-distance man, much preferring 20 and 30 kilometres if at all possible. But beggars cannot be choosers, so we turned up on the day, warmed up and got ready.

We were quite far back in the field. Peter had estimated a time of around 21 or so minutes for his finishing time and being a very low key and local race, this put us at the fastest competitor end of the list, meaning we started after the others. In essence this was a much better position for Peter to be in than starting before the others. (Ski races are held with 30-second intervals between competitors and the race is really you against the clock.) With people at regular intervals in front of us, Pete told me he wanted to know how far they were in front so that he could try to pick them off and go past them.

We were at the starting line and suddenly things took a turn for the worst for me. Peter's hearing was incredible, and he told me that he hoped the horses he could 'see' in the distance would either turn off or come past before we started. I have a dreadful fear of horses and if out walking today will cross the road and preferably hide than be within 50 metres of them. If I am in a car, I lock the doors and close the windows just in case they come near me. I had never told Peter about this phobia; there is nothing you can do about it, and, yes, I have even been horse riding to try to overcome the fear, but to no avail.

I became very tense, my shoulders tightened, my breathing increased, my pulse went through the roof. I was almost at the hyperventilation stage when I saw the horses Peter had 'seen'; they we just coming over the crest of a hill around 150 metres away. For me it was too late. Panic had already set in and I was a mess. Peter picked up on it instantly; he sensed, heard and felt something was wrong with me. He dropped the rope, turned and grabbed me by the shoulders. He looked me square in the face, a little smirk on his face, his voice calm and light, yet very serious. 'Boy,' he said (it was a term of endearment), 'get a fucking grip or we will go home. It doesn't matter, it's not important. If you are not on the ball one of us is going to get hurt, and I don't want to run into no concrete fucking bollard again today.' He said it in such a way that I half snorted, and half laughed. It cleared the air, yet my fear of the horses was still there. By the time we started the horses were still about 60 metres in front of us. Pete literally leaned on me the entire time as we went past them, my panic on the brink of coming back. As we passed them, he relaxed and said, 'For fuck sake, can we run now.'

I don't remember much of the race to be honest; my concentration was fully and completely on Peter and on guiding him to the best of my ability, ability based on very little experience. I do remember we ran reasonably well, picking off those that had started in front of us quite easily. Peter worked hard and we ran the race the way he wanted it. I was there to make sure he got around without too much drama. Towards the end of the race though my own racing instinct came in, and with a few hundred metres left I lifted the pace. Pete followed it; his knee lift was low, so I told him to lift it, and he did. We kicked the last 150 or so metres, me verbally encouraging him through the finish, him working very hard, but maintaining form and composure. Our first race was over. We ran it in just inside 20 minutes, but the time was not really important. What was important was that had we breached the plateau and proved that Peter was neither sickening for something nor was he over-trained. The race did, however, confirm that he had needed to give himself a controlled test.

We changed and started to warm down, and after we were out of earshot of the others, Peter told me in no uncertain terms that not telling him about my fear of horses was not good enough. It could potentially have created problems, and worse than that, caused injury to one of us. He was right. Peter was highly intuitive but was not a mind reader and from then on, we knew pretty much everything that was happening with each other, within certain boundaries.

On the few occasions I thought something wasn't worth telling him, he would ask a question. I couldn't lie to him, so it was not even worth trying. In order to have 100% trust there could be no secrets. Our bond strengthened because of this and Pete started involving himself in my development as a runner. We also became each other confidants, something that was extremely useful as a teenage boy, dealing with the usual embarrassing stuff you don't want to tell your parents.

There were 4 weeks left before New Hampshire, Pete was in good form, I was happy and running well myself. It was time to turn up the heat.

GOLD, NEW HAMPSHIRE

We intensified the training over that last month. I had read a lot about training after I began running with Peter. Peter had earlier had access to some fantastic coaches, such as the late John Sullivan who had trained several Olympians, including Steve Crabb. We knew that there was a month until the event. For Peter training absorption took around 10–14 days so we had only a couple of weeks to get some miles in and sharpen his speed. We ran a combination of longer runs, longer intervals and short sharp sprints over the next 10 days, then tapered and backed right off. Training will give you the foundation you need, but the rest days are what make the athlete. Those days are when the body repairs itself to become stronger.

Peter travelled to New Hampshire just after the New Year; I remained at home. He trained on snow with his Norwegian guide, Dag where the focus was nothing more than getting his technique right. You can be in the best physical shape of your life, but flaws in technique will wear down on strength. I had never even heard of cross-country skiing before meeting Pete, knew nothing about it, and could definitely not help. He had had very little time on snow in preparation for this event as focus had been on getting him physically fit. From what I understand the days prior to the events were rather intense. Dag pushing for more glide and better drive forward. Peter fighting to combine this with the fitness he had. He was not in shape for the longer events. Nothing can replace snow time as decent preparation for a 30-kilometres ski race. It's another kind of fitness, where technique rules.

I had no contact with any of the team, there was still no TV coverage and it was most definitely not high priority enough for the national newspapers to cover: nothing. It was as if the event did not exist. The people who had trained so hard, had put in so many hours of gruelling work, and had in many cases paid fares for training out of their own pockets, were invisible. It infuriated me, its infuriated people that knew me and Peter; but once more the local newspapers helped out by running articles about Peter and his successes over the next few weeks.

I finally received a card from Kathy and Pete about 10 days after the event had started. They gave a short update: Peter had won the 10 kilometres classic race and had been fastest overall in the relay event. He had gotten gold. He was World Champion. The boy did good.

I got a very short telephone call from Peter when he was at the airport. He had ended with gold in the 10, silver in the 20, and a bronze in the 30 kilometres. He was pleased but had already set up a plan to enable him to do better in the European Championships the following year.

Upon his return to London he was met at the airport by some representatives from the BBC *Sport on Friday* programme, which had run a small section on us a few months before. I have no idea as to how they got wind of his successes, as there was certainly no national coverage on the television. Peter met with David Icke and was interviewed, proudly showing off his haul. He looked dreadfully tired, having raced hard for 2 weeks, and had just stepped off the flight. But I must give him credit for remaining diplomatic. He made a strong point that the team was almost entirely self-funded, that they had travelled to America to take part in a championship event, on the same tracks, in the same arena where the able-bodied World Championships had been held in the weeks preceding theirs. He drew attention to the fact that the British team in an able-bodied world had never produced a medal at any level in winter sports, whilst the handicapped and visually impaired athletes had won a haul of gold, silver and bronze medals; *they* delivered at every championship every time. He asked directly but politely on national TV what they had to do to deserve the same recognition and respect from the Sports Aid Foundation and businesses that were renowned for sponsoring up-and-coming talent. There was no answer to be given until a short while later.

Pete around 1980 after a little success.

*Left to right: Guide Lyder Sunde, Mike Brace, Pete with the flag,
Jimmy Denton and Guide Dag Olimb.*

*Peter and Dag carrying the flag Lillehammer Olympics,
Norway 1994.*

Coming home for Bronze Dag in front Peter working hard behind.

Medal Ceremony Lillehammer 1994.

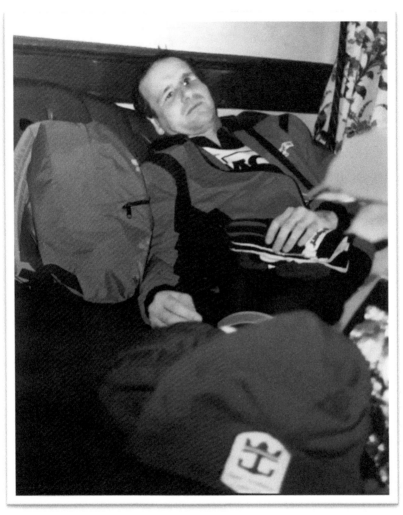

A well-deserved rest.

L-R Geoff Thompson, Fergie and Pete at a Sports Aid Foundation function around 1991-1992.

Alaska 2002. A Week later he was diagnosed with lung cancer.

My favourite and a rare pic of Pete and I together.
Windsor half marathon 1995.

Older, balder and doing it for Pete.
Me, Windsor half in 2015, 20 years after our first one together.

5

Help from Unexpected Sources

Following on from Peter's second TV appearance in early 1990 things started to move quite quickly in a positive direction with regard to sponsorship. The Royal Caribbean Shipping Company started sponsoring the British Blind Sports national team, and a travel company started giving very good prices to them for their travel, even throwing in a few free flights now and then.

More importantly for Peter was the fact that merchant bankers Samuel Montagu & Co made contact and offered him a sponsorship deal towards travel and competition costs. They asked only that he wore a badge with their name on it on his clothing. Pete was more than happy to do so, and, as at the time sponsorship and branding restrictions were not as strict as they are nowadays, he had their logo on every piece of his skiing and running clothing that was possible.

I am not sure what the amount of money was, and neither is it at all relevant, but the deal was aimed at keeping him going until after the Olympics in Albertville, France in 1992.

Peter now had sponsorship that would assist in his training and racing costs in order to prepare for Albertville. Whether Peter's assertive comments had shaken some sense into people or not I do not know; my gut tells me that people involved in the earlier broadcast featuring Peter and myself had pulled some strings in order to maybe nip an uncomfortable situation in the bud. In addition, cofounder and chair of the Metro Blind Athletics Club Mike Brace had been very active behind the scenes and Peter's successes in New Hampshire would have given a massive amount of extra ammunition for Mike to use. Mike was and is still a true diplomat for British blind sport and has always worked tirelessly to get people the recognition they deserve. He was awarded the CBE to acknowledge this.

Being politically correct was not a common phrase back then. However, you did not need to be a rocket scientist to see that Peter had a very valid point which was that the disabled athletes were outperforming their able-bodied counterparts in the Winter Games every time, without fail, yet got almost no financial backing to support what were fantastic achievements.

Others such as 'Eddie the Eagle Edwards' had risen to fame the year before when he became the first British Athlete to represent his country in ski jumping since 1929. He finished last in both the 70-metre and 90-metre events, yet became a media celebrity, even appearing on prime-time talk shows; this publicity, despite the fact that he had come last, led to him being mocked in some countries. In the aftermath of this there was even a film made. This is by no means meant to be a derogatory comment towards him; he worked hard to get to where he was. You don't just wake up and register yourself for the Olympics, and it is widely known that ski jumping is an extremely hard event to do.

But those who had really achieved, who had become champions of the world, despite being legally defined as disabled, received next to nothing. Even media coverage was limited to maybe 4 or 5 lines somewhere in the sports section of the national papers, if at all.

The important thing though was that things had moved forwards in regard to sponsorship and support.

Not long after this the Sports Aid Foundation offered Peter a grant in order to support his international efforts. His sporting CV was unquestionable, as was his total commitment to whichever branch of sport he decided to have a go at. He had to provide a wealth of information regarding costs, income and other funding but the grant was given, biannually with payments every 6 months. As a grant receiver he was invited to a banquet at the Guildhall in London, in the presence of some seriously big sporting names and also royalty in the form of Prince Edward. I was invited by Peter as his plus one, Peter deciding that I also deserved some recognition for the work I had put in with him, something I was very flattered by. It had been an incredible 6 months.

The dress code was dinner jackets and bow ties; Peters' face was a picture as he hated this sort of stuff, spending most of his days in jeans, tracksuits or training clothes. I was used to working in an office, shirt and tie was the order of the day for me so to get a little extra dressed up was fun.

I was having the time of my life. I was 18, my own running was improving, and I had been part of a fantastic journey with someone who was without doubt the best friend anyone could have; and with someone with whom I already shared the most amazing mental connection. Furthermore, the journey had already borne fruit in the way of championship medals and things were looking bright for the future. To top it all I was going to attend a fancy dinner ceremony in London's Guildhall with some of my boyhood heroes, and royalty.

Seating places were already designated; as Peter's guide I was naturally enough placed next to him, then to my right, was another man. I had never seen him before and had no idea who he was. He was extremely friendly, humbly introduced himself as Geoff Thompson, and said that he had done a bit of karate. This caught my interest, as like most boys I had always dreamed of being a black belt (I had trained at a few clubs, but never really found one that suited me), and here I was, sitting next to someone who had done 'a bit' and conversation was easy. Geoff was a nice guy and was really interested in blind sport, and the fact that Peter was a cross-country skier seemed to really catch his attention. I found out one other thing during the conversation: Geoff and his 'bit' of karate was something of an understatement.

Geoff Thompson is one of the greatest martial arts competition fighters of his generation. Five times World United Karate Organization Champion and holder of over 50 national and international titles, he had led the Great Britain team to three world team titles and was the nominated as the most valuable performer on each of those occasions. As the World Heavyweight Champion and World Games Champion, Geoff's explosive technique and style made him recognizable as the greatest point scorer in the sport's history. The karate athlete, warrior and fighter made the transition to coach and produced world, European and national champions.

In 1988, following the urban riots that swept through the UK, Geoff was a participant in the government's review of sport in the inner cities. Two years later, he was appointed to the GB Sports Council (now Sport England).

After the meal people started to mingle and Geoff made a beeline for Peter and me. With him was a young lady whom he introduced as Janice, his girlfriend. She too had done a 'bit' of karate, which is where they had in fact met. They were genuinely interested in Peter, in what he did, and how he did it. They spoke at great length about his training and asked simple yet probing questions about his physical and mental preparation. Mental preparation was something new to me. I was still naive enough to think that you trained, met up at competitions and competed. It was so far from the truth.

Whether it was coincidence or fate I do not know, but Geoff and Janice ran a training centre called Gym Excellentia in Rainham, which was about a mile and a half from where I lived with my parents. He asked Peter and myself to come along to a circuit training session, as he thought it would be beneficial to us both; we said a polite thank you and I gave Geoff my home number, and to be honest never thought more about it.

The following weekend I received a call from Geoff, asking whether we were going to come to the session the following Tuesday: we accepted. I collected Peter from home drove back to my parents' house where we decided to run the mile and a half to the gym. It was a normal training day for us; circuit training could not be that hard so we thought that it would be a good supplement to the run. The plan was to run as a warmup, do the circuit session, and then run home again as a warm down. Things did not go to plan; we really should have taken more heed to the name of the session on the training board: 'Mad Mans Mean Machine Circuit'. We ran to the gym and joined the rest of the group. Geoff welcomed us and made it very clear to everyone there: Peter was blind; I was there to help him. Watch what you do and where you go, but that was as far as the sentiment went. He then turned to us, looked us squarely in the faces and said: 'You are now just a pair of bastards like the rest of us. Let's train!'

And so, we embarked on what can only be described as the single hardest non-running-specific workout we had ever done. It was insane: 30 minutes of low, medium and high impact aerobics work. Geoff called it pyramid pattering, which was basically a set of run-on-the-spot intervals starting at 30 seconds and increasing by 15 second increments until it hit 3 minutes. Then back down the same way. Recovery was short, I am not sure it was even timed, but when Geoff felt it was time, he would shout out the next rep and then 'in 5, 4, 3, 2, 1 …' and away we went. Peter and I were runners, we were in running shape, and as hard as this was, I felt we coped quite well. The defining thing about this group though, was the camaraderie right from the start. We were not in a line; we were in a circle, close enough to be able to touch the other side. No one was in charge during each repetition; the circle had no end, and no beginning, something that the epitomized Geoff and Janice's view on training: everyone is equal in training. Whether you are world champion, or whether you are someone who just trains to stay in shape, you have a right to train, a right to feel welcome, and a right to enjoy what you do. Training is not a compulsory thing that you have to do, it is voluntary.

After the aerobic section, by which time we were already soaked to the skin, we ran upstairs to where the training apparatus was. This section depended somewhat on how many people were training. Geoff wanted no one standing idle. The machines were set to a low weight, and the aim was to carry out each exercise as fast as possible with good form for 30 seconds. In between stations there were either press up, sit ups or squats, to be carried out in the same manner: fast twitch muscle stimulation, with good form. Pete came into his own here, skiing making his upper body extremely strong. He weighed only about 10 stone 6 pounds and stood at around 5 feet 8. But he was solid. The unfit overweight 20-year-old weighing in at nearly 16 stone and nicknamed Moby Dick was long gone; it was a different person training there. Someone in his element, someone who inspired people around him, and someone that Geoff noticed.

To finish this gruelling session, we returned to the aerobic studio after the weights for cool down and core work, something we thought we were used to; once again we were wrong. The session finished, we changed out of extremely soggy clothing and put tracksuits back on, intending to run home. Lots from the group came to chat with Pete, something that suited me fine as I was having an issue standing up at the time. They were full of congratulatory words, saying he was amazing, expressing their admiration. I also thought it was fantastic. He was an inspiration, and to take part in a class like that, where it was physically impossible for me to actually guide other than by words, was an incredible feat. Geoff, on the other hand, was having none of it. He told them straight, but not in a condescending way, that Peter was there to train, he was built the same as everyone else in the room apart from being blind, and that there was nothing particularly special about it.

Personally, I thought that was a bit harsh, but Geoff explained afterwards that sympathy had no part in being the best; in individual sport there is no one to carry you if you have a bad day. No one will say you are an inspiration if you win but will shoot you down in flames if you do not perform as expected. Too many athletes with massive potential never got to where they should be, he made clear, because they neglected one extremely vital aspect of training: that aspect was the mental one.

This was a very appropriate and pungent point at the time. Peter had broken the golden rule in 1983; he had pulled out of a triple marathon in London. An event that had seen him run in the London marathon in a rather impressive 3 hours and 35 minutes, compete in a cycle marathon a short while later, and then in a canoe marathon along the Thames. In the final part of the triple, Peter gave up and pulled out of the canoe marathon, receiving a 'did not finish' comment next to his name for the first time in his sporting career. To many, this would not pose too much of an issue; to Peter who could not see how his opponents were looking and feeling during a race, and who was dependent on having good and clear information from his guide, this was a huge blow to his confidence. The seed of doubt was sown and Peter's way in looking at things also altered. He needed to feel he was in control; he needed to be in charge or at least feel as though he were in charge.

He had competed in the Summer Paralympics in New York in 1984 on the track, but despite his earlier success in the Winter games and winning the bronze medal for over 20 kilometres, he was out of his comfort zone once again. This was before my time, and I cannot really comment on what happened. I have heard stories and rumours surrounding the circumstances of what happened but will not divulge them here. Needless to say, the seed of doubt had sprouted, and once more Peter found himself stepping to the side of the sporting arena, in an Olympic final, and receiving only his second ever 'did not finish'.

During our short conversation Geoff offered us both free membership and training for as long as we wished, something we happily accepted. He then asked if Peter was interested in having a bit of help with the mental aspect of training so that Peter could release his full potential. The conversation was with Peter, and only Peter. I had absolutely no problem with this, happy just to hide anonymously on the sofa in the bar area and try to recover after the session. Needless to say, the warm-down run that evening never happened.

Pete had obviously made an impression on Geoff once again during the session, Geoff recalls:

> Pete also came to train at the Rainham Snooker club where we ran the Gym Excellentia Fitness club. He would come down with Dave (his guide) and join in the circuit training, setting the pace with his intensity and infectious will to win, commitment and determination. His special awareness was extraordinary, with many of those who participated in the sessions not even aware that he was blind, so we had to remind people at the start to watch where they were going.

Geoff Thompson was at that stage, and still is, a giver in the world of sport. He is Founder and Executive Chair of the Youth Charter which is a UK-based registered charity and United Nations non-governmental organization. It has a proven track record in the creation and delivery of social and human legacy development programmes and projects globally. The Youth Charter aims to provide young people with an opportunity through sport, arts and cultural activity to develop in life. It provides a range of initiatives and projects which can be used by educational institutions and organizations to reduce the effects of anti-social behaviour and resulting exclusion.

When asked about Pete, Geoff fondly recalls meeting him for the first time:

> I first met Pete at a Sports Aid Foundation function and upon meeting him was struck by the engaging and uncompromising nature of his character, personality and humour!
>
> Pete distracted you with his personality and you, as a result, focussed on the subject or the issue he wanted you

to engage with. He was a fantastic communicator who could tell exactly by the energy you gave, or not for that matter, who he was dealing with and, as a result, would respond or react accordingly.

We hit it off immediately as we discussed our respective competitive ambitions reflected in our social and cultural backgrounds. Our life disaffections and similarities were very evident as we spoke to 'suss one another out'. Him working me out, me working him out. Two boys from London, one black, one blind, perceived by life disabled, but empowered by sport in our respective sporting achievements.

Geoff had retired from the world of competitive martial arts and had made a switch to track running and in particular the 400-metre hurdles. He was frustrated that things were not going as he had hoped and that there was no Olympic gold in his immediate reach. Pete on the other hand was in Geoff's own words 'an exceptional medal winning athlete, and this suited his "in your face and aggressively channelled energies".'

At the time I was still actively competing, and it was not always possible for me to focus fully on Pete's needs; something that were we both aware of and something that Pete understood and accepted fully. Owing to Pete's need for training, and Geoff being the giving kind of person he is, this resulted in a series of sessions where Geoff guided Pete on the track. I believe I was there for one of these, the sight something quite head turning; Geoff standing around 6 feet 4, Peter at 5 feet 8 or so running around the track.

Again, Geoff's immense desire to win and be the best he could be, combined with Pete's desire to beat his Norwegian opposition helped two people in the same manner it had helped Pete and I. Geoff recalls:

I suppose that is ultimately what we had in common. Frustrated within our respective rebellious spirits and our challenging of authority and administrative indifference, we agreed to train together at Woodford Athletics track. I had agreed to be his track guide, which meant tying a piece of string to our respective wrists with me taking the lead and Pete close by my side.

The first was by far one of the most remarkable training sessions I was ever to experience in my entire competitive training career. Pete's sensory perception and awareness was extraordinary, and he walked and ran with a more purposeful stride and pace of intention and confidence than most people that were fully sighted.

It was from that session that I came to respect the 'sixth sense'. Pete had it in abundance. He also had an incredible vocabulary, colourful and supported by a repertoire of jokes for any occasion and any audience. Mostly blue within that very vivid imagination that engaged, captivated and motivated you.

We continued to train with Geoff for several years up until around 1993 when Geoff and Janice moved away from the area. Almost every Tuesday without fail we were there; almost every Tuesday without fail, Geoff pulled something new out of his bag of tricks; and every Tuesday without fail, Pete and I staggered exhausted from the gym and sat in the bar before I was able to drive home. The training was sometimes adapted to suit Peter specifically; other times it was just a hell on earth for everyone in the room. Janice often joined in, and I had joined the karate class run by the gym.

To try and describe someone like Pete is something many have tried and failed to do. Geoff's summary of Pete sums up the man:

Pete was a remarkable character, person and athlete. A rebellious spirit, who overcame life challenges and adversity with a discipline and focus that I place at the very highest level of sportsmen or women that I have met, encountered or trained with.

Pete was a true example of 'made in the East End'. Although his life was cut all too tragically short, when I was asked to contribute a memory of Pete, it was easy to do, easy to recount and easy to record. In sport, you meet many people from many backgrounds, beliefs and abilities. Pete stood out head and shoulders above many that I have had the privilege to know and to train with. He was the master of making the most of his God given talents and will be remembered fondly by the cheeky wit and sharp tongue that always knew when someone was simply paying him lip service. Pete literally had eyes in the back of his head and was in short a 'one off'.

We continued our circuit training in a room Peter had purposely built in his back garden. Peter had used a network of contacts and had got me into a training group with John Sullivan at the New River Stadium in Haringey. John was well known and had a proven track record of producing fine athletes from sprinters, up to middle and long distance: athletes of the calibre of Olympian Steve Crabb and other internationals such as Larry Mangleshot, and Lloyd Cowans to name but a few.

Peter knew him of old and John took us both under his wing of immense knowledge. Once again, the change in training as well as the change in the way Pete and I ran was visible almost instantly. Peter's opinion was that he wanted to give something back to me. His opinion was that, no matter how much I objected, my improvement as a runner would ultimately benefit him as well. It was a partnership we were in, not a one-way street. Besides, Peter then dropped the bombshell that he thought the training I was currently doing was wrong for the event I was aiming to run, and that he could hold his tongue no longer. He truly did always have my back.

In addition to this I had regular contact with Peter's skiing guides in Norway after he had returned home from training with them. They would tell me what areas they believed Peter needed to focus on; he could be stubborn and was not always in agreement with them, but as we never knew exactly what we were going to do until we got out of the front door, it was easy enough to come up with a training suggestion for the day. Things had progressed nicely.

The winter after taking part in the World championship event Peter competed in the European championships in Italy. Again, his results were impressive; the extra funding he had from his sponsors and the Sports Aid foundation meant he was able to travel to Norway as soon as there were skiable conditions and the tracks had been prepared. The increase in snow time meant it was much easier for him to improve where he was lacking the most in physical technique, resulting in a much more efficient use of energy. This coupled with the help Geoff Thompson had given him in regard to getting his head in a more positive place meant that Peter was now a very dangerous competitor for his Norwegian rivals. Geoff had drummed it into both mine and Peter's heads, that no matter how well you are trained, no matter how fit and fast you are, if your head is not in the right orbit before any event you will not be able to perform to your full potential. He was right; something that Peter reminded me of a couple of years later when I lost a race I maybe should have won.

At the time I met him Peter appeared outwardly confident, as though he never had a problem. I did not recognize his uneasiness about pushing hard early in a race and had thought that this was the way Peter wanted to run: hold back until the latter stages before pushing for the finish. Hindsight is a wonderful thing, and in time it became apparent that Peter actually suffered with confidence issues.

The seed of doubt was ever present and needed to be continually restrained. His Norwegian ski guides Dag and Lyder did this be giving him extremely good feedback during training. Things like 'slow down Pete I can't go any faster' are always nice things to hear and boost one's ego. For me, I had one advantage, I was faster than Peter over most distances, and in races I would increase the pace just slightly, allowing Pete to follow as if it were him making the decision. We had always agreed, however, that the final few hundred metres were where Peter would hand over the controls to me and we would always run hard to the end.

The time passed, Peter and I continued to train, our connection and bond as strong as ever. We worked, trained and ate. We spoke together daily. John Sullivan set up a schedule for us which meant that two days a week I met Peter at his house at 5.30 am for a 30-minute run before changing at his, locking the door and going to work. After work I would drive to Peter's, where another 30 minutes running was followed by John's very own circuit training session. It was nowhere near as hard as the one we had done with Geoff, but it had the same principle behind it. Tough aerobic work combined with body weight exercises.

The Olympics in Albertville France were next on Peter's agenda. He had won a bronze in the Olympics in 1984, World gold in 1990 and European gold in 1991. The Olympics held great promise. He had trained well and had remained relatively healthy throughout the entire year apart from the odd cold. He had entered the usual events of 5-, 10- and 20-kilometres classic style and also the biathlon, the first time this event had been held at a Paralympics event.

We were moving towards the late summer and early autumn and had decided with guidance from John that we should get some speed work in whilst the weather was good and seeing as my season was pretty much finished I had absolutely no issue with this. We trained mostly at Ilford and ran the odd race in Woodford to test the lay of the land. We drove to Ilford; it was warm, there were very few people around the track and only some children playing football on the pitch in the track centre. We warmed up as normal, and ran some strides, then got ready for business. Our aim was to run around 6 x 400-metre intervals with a minute recovery between each one. We wanted to run at over his normal 5-kilometre pace in order to give Pete the best chance possible in Albertville. The two Norwegian competitors, Terje Løvås and Magne Lunde, were faster than Pete over this distance, but Pete felt he had their mark over the 10- and 20-kilometre events.

The first few runs were great; we were running at around 65 seconds a lap, which was only about 4 seconds slower than Peter's personal best at that time. On the penultimate run Pete was tired, he stumbled a little coming off the bend and knocked me sideways, but regained composure. We called it a day after that interval, there was no point in slogging out the last run just for the sake of it. The last time had dropped by nearly 3 seconds. We drove home and got out of the car for a post-run cuppa and chat as was normal. Peter did not look comfortable though and was holding just above the small of his back. He guessed he had likely just twisted it a bit and thought no more of it.

We ran as usual but there was a constant niggle in his back for the next month or so; we often had to cut runs short or change what was planned, but Peter was stubborn, he was not going to rest. He needed the training; he had an Olympics to compete in just after the New Year. Neither of us thought too much about it; however, we were a little concerned that he maybe did not have the time on his feet he needed to compete in four events over a 10-day period. To top it all he came down with a stomach problem in late November making it impossible for him to be more than about 10 metres from the toilet. This remained with him for a few days and he lost a bit of weight through not eating properly, but time was still on our side and we had high hopes.

The 1992 Winter Paralympics were the fifth Winter Paralympics. They were the first Winter games to be celebrated concurrently with the able bodies Olympics and were also the first ever Paralympics at any event in France. They were held in Tignes and Albertville, from March 25 to April 1, 1992. For the first time, a demonstration event in the biathlon for athletes with a visual impairment was held. By this time Peter would be 36, and it was not clear how long he would want to continue competing.

For those that are not familiar with the term biathlon, it is basically a two-lapped ski race that involves shooting at a target once on each lap. It is extremely demanding, requiring the athlete to come from a full ski race, control their pulse and then shoot. The weapons are real, the bullets are real, and in fact the rifles are exactly the same as those carried by sighted athletes. The major difference is that the rifles cannot be carried individually by each blind athlete, and the shooting position remains constantly prone, as opposed to sighted athletes who have one shooting round standing, the other lying.

What is consistent for both blind and sighted athletes, however, is that for every shot that misses the target, the competitor has to carry out a short penalty round, which can and often does eat into any positive margin gained during the normal skiing section of the race. But we are talking visually impaired athletes here, all classes B1, B2, and B3. Most of these athletes can see nothing at all, so I struggled to understand how on earth they were going to shoot.

Peter explained it in very simple terms. A sighted military marksman set each rifle up and locked it into dead centre position. They then fired a series of shots from this locked position in order to ensure that the rifle was indeed dead centre. From here it was connected to some form of laser equipment that sent a strange electronic sound to a set of headphones every time the rifle was moved. Dead centre of the target was the lowest sound in the series. In order to make this as difficult as possible, the sounds were not in any particular scaled order. I listened once to these sounds and could barely tell them apart, so to me, this was intriguing.

The biathlon was not a new event by any means and had been a part of World and European competitions for a number of years. Peter had been competing at it in Norway for a long time. He had mixed experiences: sometimes he shot really well, other times his guides told him that nothing was safer than the target when he was shooting. Peter was never one to make excuses, but he did always say that the rifles were a lottery. They were dependent on who set them up, and more than that what had been done to them afterwards. A small kick to the tripod would move the sight from absolute zero, meaning that even the lowest sound in the range that they listened to would miss, resulting in a penalty round and lost time.

We were in Beitostølen in Norway in 1995, where they were setting the guns for a biathlon event the next day. In order to prove a point Pete picked a ready set rifle and fired off his five shots. We walked to the bullet catcher at the back of the paper target. The target showed only one hole and we all thought that he has shot badly. His guides started teasing him about how bad a shot he was, until in his own unique way Pete stopped them. He had a superb relationship with his Norwegian guides; on the snow they were his. I had enough trouble for the first year standing on the thin 7-feet-long bits of carbon, let alone trying to keep up with seasoned internationals like Pete and his guides. But, stop them he did. He uttered five simple words in his own unique manner: 'Oh for fuck sake boys'. The effect was instant; they stopped and looked at Pete who asked them to look in the bullet collector at the back of the target. They did so, and the look of sheer astonishment on their faces is something that left such an impression in my mind that I will never forget it. The look went from Pete, to the target. From the target to the collector at the back, then back to Pete. It was comical. There, nestled into the back of the collector were five small bits of metal, the bullets from each of the five shots, yet the target had one clean hole, no feathering of the edges, no other marks. Peters had managed to put five shots, through the same hole.

The events did not go as we had wished, or expected, in France. The conditions were awful, with wet snow and changing conditions in the tracks. Nordic skiing is dependent on two things other than the fitness of the competitor: one is the ability for the ski to glide forwards as you push your hip and leg through, the other is the ability of the central part of the ski to grip the snow on the kick back where you transfer your weight and propel yourself forwards.

Peter's technique was undoubtedly better than before. But he was still slightly more dependent on physical strength than were his Norwegian and Russian opponents. The tracks were wet, making waxing the skis difficult, and an amount of back slide was always going to be inevitable. Back slide results in using a lot of strength from your lower back, and, although he had recovered, his back was not 100 per cent and became sore. His results were not as we had hoped but we had time until the next ski year, and something exciting to talk about before then.

Then in 1993 Pete once again caused a little controversy. He had been invited to compete in the 'King of Norway's Cup' event in Beitostølen, a place he knew well, a place he was comfortable with. The event was a kind of world cup event in today's terms and Peter, as usual, was not just there to make up the numbers. The event over 15 kilometres, if I recall correctly, suited Peter, and he won somewhat unexpectedly.

As the medal ceremony approached, he was informed that he would not be awarded the trophy, that he was ineligible as he was not Norwegian. I don't recall the exact outcome of the discussion they held afterwards but I understand that it got quite heated and that a compromise was made whereby Peter received the gold medal, but the trophy was not awarded to anyone that year.

TO RUN OR NOT TO RUN, THAT IS THE QUESTION

The Summer Paralympics run concurrently with the able-bodied games. The same arenas and officials are used and as a rule the country that has hosted the able-bodied games are in Olympic ecstasy and turn up in their droves to watch the Paralympians compete.

The year of 1992 was already a great one for British athletics. Linford Christie had won the 100-metre Olympic final held in Barcelona in 9.92 seconds, finally shaking off the ghost of the Americans who had dominated world sprinting for so long. Pete and I had discussed taking part in the summer games on more than one occasion. I was still hopeful that I would improve enough to make at least the trials on my own merits in 1996.

We had initially thought of running the 5,000 metres and the 10,000 metres in Barcelona and had promised to have a chat about it after the Winter Games were finished. We had around 8 months to train for it and the stamina work we had done for the longer ski events was a solid foundation for building speed. I didn't relish the thought of running 12½ or 25 laps of the track, but we were talking about the Paralympics, the ultimate festival of track and field events for anyone taking part in it. I wanted to be there, to experience it, and furthermore, I believed fully that Peter had a damn good chance of winning, or at least taking a medal place.

There was another English runner who was without doubt a force to be reckoned with: a man named Bob Matthews who was in the same B1 class as Peter. Bob was already an Olympic gold medallist from earlier summer games and was a fantastic athlete. He trained only for the summer; he never competed in the Winter Games, so he maybe had an advantage. Other than that, Peter's Norwegian skiing rival, Terje Løvås, would definitely be there, and like Peter he would always meet in good condition and be in the reckoning. My thoughts were that every dog has its day. I was a track runner, Pete and I had a great connection, and I felt that after 3 years I knew how to bring out the best in him.

Peter on the other hand appeared somewhat negative to the thought. Maybe it was the fact that he was still disappointed about the Winter Games that had gone badly. Maybe the ghost of his personal

Black Dog from 1984 was still haunting him (Black Dog: a phrase used to indicate a bout of depression caused by an event or events of the past). I don't know, but for whatever reason he cut the entire thought from his mind and the summer games was never realized. In hindsight I think Peter *was* haunted by the Olympics in 1984 when he pulled to the side of the track. This I know had bothered him greatly, and I believe he had just compartmentalized this in his brain, and never dared to deal with it properly, feeling ashamed of what had happened.

The next Winter Olympic year was 1994 and the games were to be held in Lillehammer, Norway. It was a fantastic arrangement, with Pete being chosen to carry the flag at the opening ceremony. He was comfortable, it was in Norway, he was on familiar territory, in familiar surroundings. I stayed at home as before, not accepting Peter's request to go with him and be part of the team. It did not feel entirely right. I had never stood on skis and did not see how I could help. I would be there during the meals but whilst Peter was training there would be nothing for me to do. Besides, Peter had his ski guides, Dag Olimbe and Lyder Sunde, there to take care of him. This proved to be the only chance I would get to see him compete at world level, in his world, in his element, putting all the hours, days and weeks of hard work we had done together into action. He was competing in the 5- and 20-kilometre races. He was now 38 years old, and this was his fourth or fifth games. He was by anyone's standards a veteran. We had high hopes. Peter was in extremely good shape, meaning that I had to run with a much higher percentage of effort than before in training. He was strong, fit and healthy, we had added speed to his repertoire, we had done the work. Peter was ready.

Terje always spoke fondly of his relationship with Peter as both a friend and a competitor. He recalls:

> As a friend Pete was the nicest person you could ever wish to meet. He was always humble but did enjoy letting loose now and then. In fact, the entire British team were

great to be around and held a kind of magnetism for those in the same room as they were.

The guides were really well integrated in the team and because the English always met up with several competitors, all who had the same kind of personalities they were infectious, you were drawn to them, wanted to be around them.

But Peter and Terje were more than just friends, there were both fierce competitors and in the tracks no quarter was drawn.

When I first met Peter in around 1980, he was new on the scene and really posed no threat in regard to medals. I was new to the blind category of B1, having been partially sighted before, but I knew very well who Peter was. He was fun and did his best always. It was admirable that he would never just give up. As time went by and he became more accomplished as a skier and became more serious, you had no choice but to take him seriously, and when he came third in the 84 Olympics everyone on the Norwegian team pricked up their ears and paid attention.

Terje recollects:

As Peter gained motivation and confidence, I knew that at some stage he would become a real threat in the ski tracks, and when he took medals in '86 and then three in '87, I knew that he had really arrived. We, in the Norwegian team, who had really had it quite easy in the past, with only the Russians to really contend with, suddenly were faced with Peter. The guy who had made progress based on dogged hard work and guts, and who came from England above all places.

Magne and I knew each other well enough to have gotten a feel for each other, but as things were, we also knew that Peter Young never ever went to a competition unless he had trained well, and unless he thought he could do himself and Great Britain justice. I personally trained pretty much with him in my thoughts all the time, I trained to be better than him. Luckily this was often the case, but a small error on my part and it was over.

At the same time, he was humble in victory, and humble in defeat. If I beat him there was always a handshake and a word of congratulation, if he won, he always asked how my race was and asked if anything was wrong. He truly was a nice guy.

The first event was the 5-kilometre classic style. The race is conducted in exactly the same way as for the sighted competitors. In this track in the snow leading the way around the course and the technique used can be compared to that of running. The biggest difference is that with 2-metre-long skis on it is near on impossible to lift your legs. The technique here is key; it can make the difference between a good race and a bad race. You can be fit and strong, but it does not matter if you cannot get the co-ordination right and push the hips properly forwards.

Pete spent no more than 40 or so days a year on snow, He arrived in Lillehammer a week or so prior to the start of the games, and with both Lyder and Dag devoted all the time they could, picking and correcting the technique.

Pete and his guides were not like the others around him. This was deadly serious; this was business and obviously they were all extremely keen to do well. But Peter was a fun-loving person and a true believer in 'all work and no play makes jack a dull boy'. Everyone understood there was a time to be serious and a time to have fun. The British team were renowned as having the most fun with their guides, but Pete was also known as a formidable opponent on the tracks.

Racing at such a high level is stressful and fun is an absolutely necessary evil if you are not going to burn lots of nervous energy in the days leading up to an even. Peter once said: 'When the fun goes out of what you are doing, then it is time to stop.' He was always at a slight disadvantage due to the short amount of time he was able to spend on snow each year; his answer was simple, train as hard as possible when on snow, train harder still at home. His race philosophy was simple: ski your own race, nothing more, nothing less. His reasoning was: 'I am not in control of everybody else, so the simplest way around this is to be in control of myself. If I do my own race, to the best of my abilities, then I will be somewhere near the medals.'

The 5-kilometre race was first up. Peter and his guides had discussed the best way to attack this race. The big favourite, Terje Løvås from Norway, had been in incredible form in the period leading up to the championships and was without doubt the man to beat. The other Norwegian, Magne Lunde, was little more of an unknown, but like Terje and Peter, always met up at an event having put in the time and effort to be near the front.

Their tactics for the race had been quite simple. Go out as hard as possible and hold on for as long as possible. It was exactly as Peter and I had trained in the long interval sessions we had run, with me pushing the pace, and Pete holding on. Dag guided this event, but with about 450 metres to go it was apparent that Terje had set an exceptionally fast time of 15.40.6 and Peter was not going to beat it. As per the rules Dag stepped to the side with about 150 metres to go, urging Peter forward. Pete used his upper body and core strength to 'double tuck' his way forwards: keeping his feet firmly planted in the tracks, digging his ski poles into the snow, then using his entire upper body and stomach to pull forward. He finished in 16.23.2, some 43.4

seconds behind Løvås but 4 seconds in front of the Russian skier Kouptchinski and gaining second place at that stage. The big four of the two Norwegians, the Russian and Peter were where they always were: at the top, fighting for just three medals.

With one main opponent left in the tracks a medal was secured, the question remained as to which colour it would be. Gold was gone, it was between silver and bronze, and between Peter Young of Great Britain and Magne Lunde of Norway.

Magne came into the arena with an almost identical time to Peter's; it was going to be very close. It was at this point that the minor flaws in Peter's technique proved to be his downfall. Lunde crossed the line with a total finishing time of 16.22.9 seconds to take the silver and relegate Peter to the bronze medal. He was 3/10ths of a second in front, over a distance of 5,000 metres. Peter had done it, had done extremely well, and not even in his favourite event. The hard work had paid off.

In a post-race interview Pete said: 'Dag did his usual perfect job of guiding, and luckily I had a day where the technique managed to come good for me. But it was tough, you don't get anything for free at this level, so yes, it was hard.' This was Peter in a nutshell, ever thankful to his guides.

His final race was the 20 kilometres, something that as a rule was Peter's strongest event. In Lillehammer this consisted of two laps each of 10 kilometres. Guide changes were allowed as often as needed and Dag and Lyder shared the job, with Dag taking the first 10 kilometres, then changing as they started the second lap. Peter started more cautiously. Whether it was due to tiredness after the 5 is not clear; maybe he was just aware that 20 kilometres is a long way.

The same four, Lunde, Løvås, Young and Kouptchinski, were once more fighting for three medals. The conditions were good, the tracks newly prepared, the training was done. Peter skied well, both physically and technically, but this time it was not enough to secure a medal. Løvås was unstoppable in this Olympics winning the 5, 20 and 30 kilometres.

Peter finished a fair way behind the two Norwegians and the Russian and people suspected that this was due to basically a bad day. Gerald Sinstadt happened to be commentating the event for BBC2 and said that Peter had not had the best of days. Peter, Dag and Lyder had been following Terje Løvås's results and found that earlier in the season he had been winning these events by 2 or more minutes. In this instance he won by just over 40 seconds. Lunde and Kouptchinski had had the race of their lives; on a normal day, Peter would have challenged strongly for one of the other two medals. On analysis, Peter had skied a technically very good race. The waxing of the skis was good, and the course, although hard was not the issue. Bottom line was that the three who beat him had on the day been better. Nothing more; there were no excuses. We had trained and prepared well but, on the day, Peter had not been fast enough.

For me, 1994 was a good year. My own training was coming on in leaps and bounds. My times were coming down and I was seriously starting to think that I really could be good at this. The Essex County Championships were held on May 16 and 17 May that year at the Terrence McMillan stadium in Newham. It was a track I knew well; it was the home of Newham and Essex Beagles, my club. But by this time, I had lost a lot of contact with pretty much everyone there. I ran in the club matches and turned up when asked to run British league matches. I felt more comfortable at that level and as long as I was running B races was fine. I never had a great deal of success and think that third was the best I was ever placed in one of these races, but the experience was important. Preparation for the Counties was going okay; I felt I was running well and clocked a semi decent run at the first open event in Woodford Green about a month before the event was due to start. I needed another race at least and with the first club league match a week or so away I looked forward and felt positive about my chances. I had been training for 800 metres and when I was told that I was to run 1,500 metres instead was a little shocked. Those selected for the 800 had been consistently slower than me and I really did not like the 1,500 metres at all. I spoke with Peter on the phone when I found out. I knew what I wanted to do, I had an impression what John Sullivan was going to say, but for me, Peter's opinion was what really mattered.

Peter answered the phone in his usual happy manner, then caught on something was wrong. There was no hiding from it. I explained what had happened, what had been said, and his answer was as I had expected. He was not best pleased and told me in straight talk that I was an idiot if I ran over distance so close to the Counties. For me on that day, his word was sacrosanct. I rang John telling him what Peter and I had discussed. John agreed and made the call to the team manager telling him sorry, but I was not going to be at the meeting. It did not go down particularly well, and I felt a weight off my shoulders straight away. I sounded big headed, selecting what events I was or was not going to race in for my club without having ever really proved what level I might be at. Once more Pete stood strongly in my corner.

The day of the County Championships arrived. Pete could not be there for the heats as he was playing a county cricket match at Lords but called me with a pep talk before, he left. His advice was very simple to follow: 'Don't get boxed in, keep from being right on the inside by the curb, and get the hell involved from the start!'

The heats were late in the day, the weather reminiscent of our second run together with rain bouncing off the track. It was not cold but there was a slight breeze making the rain sting as we came into the home straight. I ran a decent race. Kept out of the way as Pete had told me to for the first lap and tried to follow the breakaway group with about 300 metres to go. Coming into the final straight I was lying third. There were only going to be two heats so qualifying was the first two in each heat plus the four fastest losers. Being in the first heat I had no idea how fast the second heat would be. I wanted one of the automatic places.

I accelerated but it looked as though I was going to run out of track. I don't know what happened or where it came from, but it was almost as though someone suddenly pushed me in the back, forcing me past the other two. I won the heat just and qualified directly for the final the next day.

I rang Peter the Sunday morning to tell him; he sounded groggy and admitted that there had been a few gins after the cricket. Regardless of that he was definitely coming to watch the final that afternoon, and could we collect him on the way. I rang the doorbell; Peter answered looking a little worse for wear and stinking like a distillery. He was somewhat hungover, and I could see that he really did not fancy running the warmup with me. But he knew it was important to me so took our rope with him. He was that type of person, a promise made is a promise to be kept. His opinion was that if it was important to me, it automatically made it important to him. I am not sure what would have happened that day had Peter not come along to support me, but I don't think my brain would have been as fully on the race as it needed to be.

During the warmup he got given a rundown of those in the final, their lane placings and their qualifying times. His mind was like an encyclopaedia at times, and he remembered a lot of the names from before. Generally, it was the same people to contend with at the Championship events, especially at County and Southern County Level. I had been given lane 4, which is a perfect lane draw, and Pete told me yet again to get stuck in from the start, that there was nothing and no one there that should bother me.

The race started quite quickly but settled down and bunched up after around 200 metres. Initially I was right at the front but eased back as I did not want to lead. At the bell I was around 10 metres off the pace. Usually I never heard anything at all when I ran other than the timekeeper shouting the lap times but with 300 metres to go, I heard Peter bellow at me, his voice unmistakable, and his words sadly indistinct.

Coming off the final bend I was in fourth place, closing fast, Pete screaming at me to stay where I was and not try to go around anyone.

A gap opened, I was in third, still closing fast. This time, I did run out of track, finished third and missed coming second by around 1/100 of a second, and first by not more than half a second or so. I was pleased, I had run well. Granted, not the best tactically, but I had run a best time of under 1 minute 54. Things had gone well.

Pete wanted to come for the warm down with me, something I thought was nice. I was buzzing, high on adrenaline and the result had not yet really sunk in. We hadn't gone far when I asked Pete what he thought. His answer was not what I was expecting at all. He let loose with a barrage at me telling me that I had thrown the race away because I was scared. He told me I was scared of running fast, scared of running from the front, and scared of the names of the guys that beat me. I was totally shell-shocked. Hurt by the fact that I had run a personal best and yet I was still on the receiving end of his outburst. But, at the same time, I knew Pete was right on the money as usual. I had backed off the pace at the front as I did not want to lead, and I had stayed off the pace when the guy who won took up the running. He had a best time a second or better than my own. After this, I usually listened to the advice Peter gave about almost everything. However, there were a few instances when I did not. One of these was to put a huge strain on our partnership only a short time later.

A STORM BREWING

The rest of 1994 was pretty uneventful. I reduced my 800-metres time by another second or so and Peter and I continued to train. There was some worry about financing Peter's training if he was going to compete in the Nagano Winter Olympics in Japan in 1998. Peter would need a lot of training and this was expensive. He would be 42, a veteran in the world of sport, and there were some good athletes on the way up. Peter knew he would need more practice on snow, and sufficient time to prepare in Japan. He decided to go for it, as usual never shying away from a challenge, on the condition that we managed to get some form of financial support in addition to that he received from the sports council.

In the meantime, Mike Brace had managed to secure the first international, British Blind Sports half marathon to be held in October 1995, which would coincide with the running of the Windsor half marathon in October.

Peter was at first unsure about this. The preparation would mean that we would have to increase the mileage we trained, something he was worried would destroy my own season. Personally, I saw no problem, so after agreeing we accepted the invitation. I was going to run my first half marathon, 13.1 miles at the end of a summer season where I would run mainly 800 metres events. It seemed daunting.

But first, the County Championships were my target. They were very local being held in Barking, my home borough. I was confident after the year before. I had run faster; felt I was in shape and had Peter's words from the year before still very much to the forefront of my mind. I was, however, slightly concerned that we had been late starting speed work that year, but thought that when you get to the finals, it is often more tactical, and I would probably be okay.

For some reason that year there was a lower entry for the senior event, and they ran it as a straight final, as there were only ten in the field. I ran well, sticking to the front and accelerating along the final half of the back straight. Coming off the final bend I was in a great position, on the shoulder of the lead two, with space to move through. This time, when I tried to accelerate, there was nothing in the tank, I faded and came in fourth. I was quite disappointed, but once again Peter was on hand, telling me that the race was run tactically very well from what he could see. I was basically a little short on speed. But this boded well for the rest of the season, and for my dream of trying to enter the AAA championship the year after.

We were training a few days later when I had a reoccurrence of an ankle injury, I had sustained in around 1992. My ankle was slightly unstable and rolled, tearing more of the medial tendons. This put me out for a week or so, but my ankle recovered well. We continued training afterwards with no adverse effects but decided to come off the speed a little in order to give it a chance to repair and strengthen. Pete used his mass of contacts in the athletics world and had got me to a fantastic physio back in 1991. This guy basically kept me going.

I had entered the Southern Counties Championships at Crystal Palace the same year. I will not go into too much detail but events at the race saw me injure the ankle again and fall during the race. Events directly after this saw me in a heated discussion with some members of the Beagles club and I decided it was time to cut ties. I resigned and decided I would run non-affiliated for a while and look at joining another club later. The most pressing issue though was the ankle. More trips to the physio showed that there was a distinct weakness in the tendons, meaning that the ankle would remain unstable despite supports, etc. Running 800 metres was no longer a viable option for me. My ankle would basically not take the work of being up on toes and running at speed anymore. So, after sitting with Pete and discussing it, I took the hard decision to 'retire' competitively for myself. It was a blow to my self-esteem and self- confidence. My dreams had gone up in smoke and once more Peter was there with wise words and support.

He gave me a get out if I wanted it. He saw no reason for me to run anymore with him, when he felt it would be all one sided. I would be giving, and he is taking. Everything would revolve around Peter. For me this was never an option. I may have had to retire for myself but providing my ankle would hold running slower than I normally could, I would continue. Every cloud has its silver lining, the silver lining here was that all of my time and energy would be directed at working with Pete. Japan now had a new meaning, as did the Windsor half marathon. We could now train specifically for this without the question of how this would influence my own season.

6

Training and more help

During the time I had been running with Peter he had often travelled to Norway in order to train with his ski guides. These trips were predominantly in the winter months, depending on when the snow came to the areas where they lived. He also took part in the Ridderrennet ski festival held around March or April in a mountain resort called Beitostølen, situated in eastern Norway at around 900 metres above sea level.

These trips were fun end-of-season affairs, and although there were some hard and serious races going on, it was not a championship event. The British groups travelled from far and wide, their numbers ranging from 10 up to 50 or more. It is here that Peter first learned to ski way back in 1974, it is here he fell in love with his sport, and he made a point of attending each year regardless of his fitness level at the time. The gatherings were a time to meet friends, ski during the day, and enjoy letting your hair down in the evenings.

He had mentioned after one of these trips that the Metro Sports Club group needed more sighted helpers during these weeks. They were somewhat intense with lots of assistance needed. In 1995 I was asked if I would go along to help, and not least of all to ski. I had never been skiing before but had seen Peter on the TV so had a rough idea as to what it was. I agreed to go, and my ticket and accommodation was covered by Metro Sports.

We met at Heathrow early in the morning, checked in and had an amount of time to kill before our flight left for Oslo Fornebu at twenty past ten. I knew most of the group: Jimmy Denton, a B3 at that time, Kenny Bodden, a fantastic character known for bursting into song at the first available chance, and Peter Longgate, a drinking buddy of the others. There were others there too. Mike Brace had organized the whole thing along with his wife Maureen. It was quite intense from the outset: baggage needed to be moved from the check-in desk to the oversized luggage hall, and people needed to get through passport and security control; the sticks that they would normally use were packed away, as guides were there.

In Pete's world, when there was no skiing and no training plus time to kill, there was only one place for them to go in order to make time pass. The pub.

We sat at a pub after going through to the duty-free area, and by quarter to eight that Sunday morning, Peter and the guys were well into their second pint. I found out afterwards that Norwegian beer is more pilsner based, and not something they actually used for any other reason that getting drunk. I tried to avoid this by drinking orange juice, but that was really not going to happen, so I sat trying to look like I was enjoying my pint, when I really wanted to lie down and sleep.

We eventually got onto the plane for our flight. And after a short 2-hour trip, where I slept pretty much the entire way and the others drank gin and tonic, we arrived at Fornebu. I had never been to Norway before; there were a lot of people at the airport, lots of baggage and lots of skis. Our group I think was around 18 or so both sighted and unsighted so those that were not visually impaired were tasked in grabbing the luggage as it came through. We matched the luggage to the owner and in a long procession of people and trolleys headed outside to try and find the buses that were going to take us onwards.

The next leg of the trip was a lengthy one. Four hours through the mountain roads of eastern Norway, the light fading even though it was only around half past three in the afternoon. It was cold as well I remember, and the duty-free gin and tonic purchased at Heathrow was flowing freely. Kenny started singing, and soon the entire bus was following his lead. It was a great atmosphere. The more the drink flowed, the more risqué the songs became, but it never really got out of control and the bus driver did not seem to be at all distracted. I was really unsure as to what I should do with myself. I felt like an extra wheel; that I was in the way.

After what seemed an eternity, we arrived at Høysfjellhotell in Beitostølen. The hotel was set at the end of the road with views over the slalom hill. The scenery was like a picture postcard with rolling mountains and snow, lots of snow. The temperature was not too cold but well under zero. There were a lot of people around at the time, so check-in took a while. Then there was time before dinner to mingle and have a beer for those that had not already had their fill.

It was at dinner I first realized what Peter had meant about the sighted helpers being very necessary during this week. We needed to navigate our way through other guests to tables, find seats and make sure that everyone was there. It was a very pleasant time of the day, sitting together and sharing our meal.

Meals were pretty much on a buffet basis, and again the learning curve for me here was steep. People needed to know what was on offer, we needed to fill plates as well and make sure the plates managed to get back to the tables with their contents intact and not on the floor.

Some of the guys had a system for eating: vegetables at a certain place on the plate, potatoes at another, meat somewhere else. Other just worked their way through the food until they could find no more. It was really fascinating in a strange way. To be fair, there was very little mess, and very little spillage. It was somewhat incredible. The sighted helpers for want of a better word all mucked in together and there was no one who helped just one person. It was, however, hectic and there were not many meals where the food we put on our own plates was still warm when we finally got to eat it. It did not bother me. I loved being there, being immersed in the atmosphere and environment, and surrounded by a group of people that I really felt I connected with and belonged to.

After dinner people met their guides for the week, if they had not already arranged to meet a guide, they were familiar with. The natural progression was either to break the ice or to reacquaint themselves with their guide, which naturally meant they generally headed to the bar. I was by this time exhausted after the day spent travelling, so gave Peter the second room key so he could get in later, and I headed off to bed. I do not know what time he staggered in; I was sleeping heavily and did not hear him come in.

The next morning, I was woken by Pete wandering back from the toilet. The room had coffee and tea making facilities and Peter was in the throes of making a couple of coffees for us before we headed down to breakfast. Pete had said that he would be taking me to someone he knew in order to get me fitted out with skis. He had given me a racing suit to wear so that I at least looked the part and said he had hoped I would be able to take the Ridderrennet race of 20 kilometres by the end of the week.

I opened my eyes I reached for my watch to get an idea of the time. The watch was on the bedside cabinet between the two single beds in our room. I reached for the glass of water that was there too and as I lifted the glass heard a clinking sound. Looking across I saw two eyes staring at me through the water. At first, I thought they were in the water but realized they were on a handkerchief on the tabletop. I gasped and most likely said a choice word or two. Peter cracked up laughing at first, then realized that in all the years we had been running together, that subject had never come up. What did he do with his eyes at night? I had seen him clean them during a run, but thought that otherwise they stayed in. I found out in a rather funny way that he took them out, in the same way that others take out their teeth at night. In hindsight, it is quite strange that, despite having little prior knowledge of the blind world before running with Peter, it had never crossed my mind to ask what it was like to be blind. The only thing I knew from Peter was that he saw nothing. He couldn't describe light and dark, he couldn't really describe colour; the things we sighted people and those in the B2 and B3 classes of athletes took for granted, Peter had no concept of. After this first morning Pete was careful not to leave them in plain sight again. I really don't know why, I never thought to ask, and Peter never said anything more about it.

The other thing that struck me with Pete was how at home he was in Norway. From what I know now, his verbal Norwegian was appalling despite travelling to the country for 20 years, but it was good enough to say beer, thank you and to understand his guides if they struggled to find the English words they were looking for. He was naturally fluent in all words dealing with swearing, as is most often the case for most Englishmen when learning a new language.

He skied well that week, winning a race or two, and getting beaten in others. Racing was done with the utmost sincerity, and everyone gave their all. After-ski, however, was on a totally different level, starting at some time around three in the afternoon and continuing late into the evening, only being interrupted for dinner. It didn't take long for Pete and Kenny to start entertaining in the manner they knew best. Pete being loud, confident and jovial, always had a group of people around him, and seemed to know just about everyone there in the bar. Kenny sat on the chair with a guitar he had behind the bar and crooned classics such as 'The Boxer' by Simon and Garfunkel, as well as 'Where Do You Go to My Lovely?' by Peter Sarstedt. As the evening drew on, and a few more beers were drunk and the alcohol took effect, other not so well-known classics like 'Seven Drunken Nights' and 'A is for Arsehole' were top of the list, as well as the children's song 'Roll Me Over in the Clover', sung with a somewhat more adult audience in mind. It was clear that both Pete and Kenny were extremely comfortable in Beitostølen; they knew everyone, and everyone knew them. The English team was well and truly in their element, competing and training hard by day, and partying just as hard by night. The week was passing too swiftly and the last evening drew near.

The last evening saw us drop in on a neighbouring hotel where there was a cabaret artist whom the guys knew very well. He had just arrived in Beitostølen and Pete had not bumped into him yet. So off we went to the Bergo Hotel.

Sitting there in the Bergo Hotel waiting, I noticed a young lady of about my age, with medium-long blonde hair, carrying two trays of empty glasses. Peter knew her and tried to introduce me. As she walked past, she stumbled, sending the two trays flying through the air and the empty glasses smashing in a cascade all over the floor. I helped her pick them up and got speaking to her a little later. But time had crept up on us, and we were due to leave; no time for a holiday romance this time around.

The next morning, we were on the road early again making the 4-hour return bus journey to Oslo. The guys were back on the gin, or at least what was left of it, and most of them were still three sheets to the wind from the night before. I was tired; it had been hard work but also a lot of fun, and an extremely enlightening week that had given me a much better insight into Peter and his world. It was truly something to behold, something you had to see and be a part of in order to understand it on anything other than a superficial level. By the time we got back to Oslo I already had my name down on next year's list.

Otherwise the year of 1995 really all got jumbled together as so much happened at the same time. The training and such are not given in correct chronological order, but the events are correct and showed people in both good and bad lights.

We spoke with John Sullivan at the next training session after I decided to stop competing for myself. He was saddened by the physio advice but had seen my ankle break down and knew how painful and demoralizing it was for me so could do nothing more than accept the decision. We then told him we wanted some specific training for the half marathon in the time we had left. It must have been late June by this time, so time was running out for us.

John set to work almost at once. The training was brutal, and even harder than the winter training we had done. It was warm that year and we trained on the track twice a week. For those that are not familiar the track gets hot with the heat bouncing off the track surface. The majority of tracks are also in a kind of bowl, either recessed into the ground or built up with stands surrounding them.

The track work was hard right from the start. We were running with me coming off an aborted season and Pete already training for the winter. Training consisted of two days of short repetitions with a short recovery, so 16–20 x 300 or 400 metres with 30 seconds between each was not uncommon. A 30-second recovery is fine until you have done a few runs. Then the accumulative effect starts to catch up and by the time you get to halfway it is hard to get any kind of control over your breathing. Heart rates were not monitored then, but it would have been interesting to see how high they got.

John followed every single interval as he always did, timing both repetition and recovery. Most of the time it was warm, but on those occasions when it was raining, he was still there every interval, along with us. John loved his coaching and his athletes never paid towards their training; all he asked or expected was that people took it seriously.

The third interval session each week consisted of longer repetitions of between 800 and 1,200 metres. There were fewer of these, only around 8–10. Recovery was short; if John was feeling generous that day, we would get maybe 2 minutes, but most of the time recovery was not more than 90 seconds. He did have expectations though, and if they were slower than he wanted us to run, he would give a clear message to speed up.

The other three training days were all about miles. I guess we were running somewhere around 35 miles in addition to the track. The longest run was in Hainault forest on Sunday mornings. It was never usually fast and lasted for around 14 miles or so.

Running alongside the training for the half marathon was something else that was equally exciting. After stopping karate training when Geoff and Janice moved from the area, I had started training at another club under Glen Moulds in Dagenham. The

Kenshinkai Shotokan Karate Club was founded in 1972 and is one of England's longest running clubs. It is now based in Suffolk.

Glen was an ex-policeman when I got to know him. One evening after we had trained a group of us went to the pub. Glen had seen us running and wanted to know more about it, so I let him know about what Peter did and the trouble we had gaining sponsorship for him.

The Japan Paralympics in Nagano were 3 years away; there were some other events in the meantime, but Pete knew that 1998 was his last shot at Paralympic gold. He would be 42 and a veteran in the event. His only option was to get as much time on snow as was possible, that is to chase the snow when it arrived in Norway, but this meant time off work, which in turn meant loss of earnings. The Sports Aid Foundation grant had been reduced a little and would not cover very much.

I was at work the next day when Glen rang me on my office number. He wondered if I could meet with him at lunchtime in order to listen to an idea he had. At that time, I was teaching a couple of evenings a week and thought it might be some kind of idea to get more students into the dojo (a room or hall in which martial arts are practised).

Glen and a group of others were delivering flyers and I met him and his wife, Julie. Glen said that Julie had come up with an idea over breakfast that morning: maybe the club could help Peter gain sponsorship. They outlined the idea of a Karatethon, a 12-hour sponsored karate training session. There was a lot of work to be done as we would be starting from scratch: no idea where to start, who to speak to, or how to go about trying to get this thing up and running.

To be honest, I am not sure of the date it was to be held but believe it to be around late October or November of 1995.

So, we spread ourselves thin. Peter did his bit and got in touch with the local newspapers expressing his thanks. Glen used a network of contacts to find premises and called on instructors who would most definitely be needed; there was no way that one man could teach solidly for 12 hours.

I, for my part did what I could. I managed to get hold of Eugene Gilkes from Newham and Essex Beagles, a really lovely and humble man who had competed alongside Daley Thompson in the Olympics. He was a real team-player and often turned out for the club when asked. He was thrilled to be asked and gave a rather motivational talk on training and preparation for events. It was highly interesting to hear from someone who had been there, with the best in the world, at the Olympics.

I also managed to contact Paul Alderson, one of Geoff Thompson's students who had won the World Karate Championships in his weight. He was on the way to an event but stopped in for an hour and taught some different fighting techniques to us all.

The amount of work prior to the Karatethon was massive: we needed to organize sponsorship forms and get people to sign up; we needed to keep costs down as low as possible, and at the same time feed people. Glen, Julie and I spent at least two afternoons a week on the telephone to potential sponsors, whether they were supermarkets where we asked for food, or sports drinks producers asking for a few bottles here and there. In time it started to come together. I still did my day job, taking annual leave to work on the Karatethon, Glen and Julie made this as an inaugural part of their day, and I was still running with Pete. We all spread ourselves way too thin.

At the same time all of this was going on, I had started seeing a girl from the club. She was a couple of years older than me, trained karate and lived not too far from the dojo. Although she was not as involved in the planning of the event, she was, like everyone else, going to spend 12 hours of her Sunday trying to earn her sponsorship money for someone she knew little about. Peter came to the dojo one evening and spoke a bit about what he did and how, but his time was also limited, and he never got there as often as he wished.

Training for the half marathon was well underway. Both Peter and I had dropped a lot of weight. Not because we wanted to, but the training was intense, and getting enough food was hard. In the 1990s there was very little known about sports nutrition for runners; electrolyte and isotonic gels and drinks were still a few years away from being realized. In addition, we both worked full time and I also taught a couple of evenings a week. On race day I had dropped back to 9stone 1lb, Peter was just around 10 stone. One thing is for sure though: we were fit.

It was during this training period that I came face to face with two incidents that showed how narrow-minded and downright stupid and ignorant some people can be. The first happened on a training run. We ran late and it was dark, but we had reflective vests on and were visible. The road we were running down had extremely narrow pavements due to people parking with their wheels on the curb. Although we could have managed to run along the pavement, the road was near on a mile long, so seeing as it was normally quiet for traffic, we decided to run in the road. We had done it many times over the previous 5 or 6 years without issue, and people had, as a rule, read the back of the reflective vests Gerald Sinstadt had given us and kept a decent distance. This one night proved to be somewhat different and shook me up a little.

As we were running a car came behind us. The music was thumping so loudly that even I heard it a long way off. The lights were on full beam despite the streetlights being lit and giving a decent light. The car came up behind us fast and sat only a few metres behind us. It was irritating and there was nowhere for us to go so I stopped and pulled Peter into the side of the road so the car could pass.

The person driving was about my age I guess, maybe a little younger. He wound down his window as he got level with us, but instead of saying thanks as most drivers did, he called us a pair of fucking queers holding hands running down the road in running tights. This was not the first time we had heard this. It was something that occurred at least once a week, if not more, and it never really bothered us. In some respects, I can see how people could think this. The rope we used was short, not more than maybe 20 centimetres long from end to end, and it was dark blue, making it invisible in the dark when we were both holding it.

He drove past, then pulled into the side of the road; Pete and I ran past as normal never even acknowledging he was there. We hadn't got far when he was behind us again; no music playing but revving up close behind us. It was intimidating, distracting, and downright dangerous. Once again, we stepped to the side, once again he hurled abuse as he went past. Peter's patience was wearing thin and he asked the guy why he didn't just grow up and fuck off. Then everything happened fast.

The car stopped in front of us and the driver's door opened. The guy got out and, in the streetlight, I saw he was carrying something in his hand. It was not until he slammed the thing into the ground that I realized he was carrying a metal baseball bat and he was extremely angry. It was a sticky situation: we could turn and run the other way but were never going to outrun a car; we could get behind the cars on the pavement and hope he would go away, but at that particular spot there was no space for two people to pass between the cars. I decided that seeing as I was sighted it might be easier for me to defuse the situation and I pushed Peter into the gap between the cars. The guy was coming forwards and swinging the bat. Whether he meant to be as menacing as he appeared, I really cannot comment, but it did not take much for me to work out that getting hit by a baseball bat by someone so full of rage was never going to end well. Peter stood still and I sensed that he was trying to get an idea as to what was going on. I was looking at the bat, half-paralysed by fear and adrenaline.

Everything went into slow motion for a while and I remembered something Glen had been demonstrating about defending yourself against somebody with a weapon; as the guy swung and missed, I stepped forwards and managed to lock both his elbows, rendering the bat useless. There was a struggle, he screamed in pain and the bat fell.

By this time there were a few curtains twitching and a set of blue flashing lights came down the road; someone had called the police, something I was very thankful for. They stopped, asked what had happened, and then saw the guy clutching at his elbow, the bat on the floor. For one moment I really thought I was going to get in trouble, that they thought I had attacked him, but someone came out from a house and explained what had happened.

Peter, being the man, he was, spoke briefly with the police and said he had no intention of pressing charges. Baseball bat man was bundled into a car, and Peter and I continued our run, a little cold and shaken up maybe, but both in one piece. I had a sore rib for a while, but it would have been a lot worse had the bat struck me or Peter. It was the 1990s, homophobia was maybe at an all-time high, and homosexuals not as widely seen or accepted as they are today. None the less, the fact that someone had come at us with a baseball bat and had to my mind fully intended to use it was shocking and stayed with me for a while, every time a car came up behind us.

As part of the preparation for the Windsor Half Marathon John had said we should race as much as possible. The distances varied, and we never tapered the training down for a race. We took these as really hard blow outs to clear the lungs and break the monotony that either intervals or mileage can cause

One of the favourites runs at the time was the Old Eastway Cycle Track in Chingford. Sadly, this closed in 2006, but before then the runs were at least one Tuesday a month. The distance was 5 kilometres, made up of three 1-mile laps with a 300-metre finishing straight off the main loop. The event was always well attended and there were always decent runners there. One of John's boys, Larry Mangleshot, who I had trained with for many years, had broken through internationally and was the current master of the course. I don't think he was beaten in about 10 years and had clocked an impressive time of 14.21.

Three laps suited Peter and me in this particular instance, as we could get an idea of how we were doing in regard to endurance. We had trained at no real speed, as pure speed work for the half marathon was not something John had prioritized. He was looking at speed endurance: the ability to settle into a pace and maintain it for a long period of time. We were not expecting to win the half marathon; the record on the Windsor course at that time was around 64 minutes.

The race at the cycle track started as most do with a huge surge. Peter and I were caught up in it but settled into the pace that Peter wanted to run at. This was our way, always. Peter set a pace he wanted, I might tweak it slightly if we were a little outside the range where we wanted to be, but my job was to guide so that he got the easiest possible route. He needed to relax and trust me especially at speed. This was how it always had been from the very first race; at least, until the last few hundred metres, when he gave me free reign to increase speed and kick towards home. Hopefully we would pass more people than passed us.

The pace Peter set was fast for us. We had spoken about running hard, and in this case, it was to start hard then hang on when things started to get tough. According to an old diary, we clocked the first lap in 5.32, which was really moving for Peter. I felt okay at this speed, having a mile best of around 4.10, but was still working hard. My brain was working overtime trying to read what was happening in front and around us. At that sort of speed things happen quickly and there is not much time for the guide to see, consider and respond in order to make a decision about what to do. The second- and third-mile times were somewhat slower, as expected, at 6.01 and 6.03 but we had latched onto a group of runners and had been racing alongside them. That is the beauty of large field races such as at the Eastway and the majority of other events that are around today. There are generally distinct groups of runners, of differing standards, but always some runners of around the same level as you, meaning that you never run alone, and often help to bring the best out of each other.

We were part of a group of maybe five or six others, all working hard and trying to gauge how much faster the others might be able to go. Peter and I maybe had a small advantage in that there were two of us, and many I think, believed that getting two of us really moving would take a little longer than it did. It really was a race within a race. As we came off the final section of the last lap and into the finishing section, Peter dug in deep as I slowly tried to do the same. It was really nip and tuck between us and with one other guy, and as we got inside the last 100 metres or so encouragement from the spectators was loud enough to be heard clearly.

Then the second of the incidents I referred to earlier occurred. There was a clear, shrill female voice, obviously cheering on the person who was running next to us at the time, and who I was determined we were going to beat. I can almost remember what was said word for word: 'Come on don't let the blind guy beat you.' We edged in front: 'No, no, don't get beaten by a blind man, oh no you are getting beaten by a cripple.' We crossed the line first. He crossed a stride or so behind us. Our finishing time was 17.36; we were very pleased, the endurance was there, we still had some speed, John had once again set us on the right track.

Athletics is a great sport. There is never any trouble. There was never any equipment stolen or bags ransacked back then (I can't speak for today). At the end of the race, everyone congratulated everyone else. We had all run the race; we had all run as best as we could at that given point in time. Regardless of whether you won or came last you always shook the hands of those around you. This day was no different. Peter and I were gasping for breath and trying to navigate away from the finishing tunnel, when the guy we beat came over and shook hands saying well done. He said he thought Peter was amazing and that we had run well. We changed back into tracksuits and as we found space to start our warm down the chap we had beaten came over and asked if he could join us. Again, this is something unique to athletes, you warm up with an opponent, and warming down with them is not uncommon. It's a good way to find out things that happened during the race.

As we jogged, we chatted about Pete, his skiing, the Windsor Half Marathon. The guy made an apology for the person that had shouted out as we neared the finish. Peter had not paid that much attention to it; it was something we were kind of used to by now after running around the streets of Barking and Dagenham for 6 years! At least this time there were no baseball bats!

 Peter waved it off, said it happens and that people cannot help being ignorant. Sometimes, he said, people are embarrassed, as they don't see someone who is disabled as being a worthy winner and see themselves as superior due to not being disabled. The guy was really apologetic and made a joke that Peter had just run 17.36 for a 5-kilometre race, and God help anyone who said he was disabled. But the comments that had been shouted had obviously touched a raw nerve with him, and as we jogged past a group of people, he asked us to stop. So, we did.

He went into the crowd and came back with a woman. She was about Peter's age I guessed, smartly dressed, and the guy introduced us to his wife. He then proceeded to tear a strip from her in front of a lot of watching eyes. He made it clear: firstly this 'cripple' happened to be an international athlete; this blind guy had run faster than him on the day, that there was no concession given at the start and that he started on an equal par with everyone else. He also made it very clear that his wife had been highly offensive and that he too was offended and embarrassed by her behaviour and comments. Then the bombshell: he demanded that she apologize to Peter right there, right then, in front of the people who were obviously watching. She did so sheepishly and rather flush in the face. We finished our warm down together and that was that, it was never mentioned again. I would, however, have loved to have been a fly on the wall when those two got in the car on their way home that evening.

THE WINDSOR HALF MARATHON

The time left before the autumn and the Windsor Half Marathon went pretty much without incident. We worked, we trained, we ate, and we slept. Glen, Julie and I continued striving towards the Karatethon, which was to be held not long after the half marathon; everything was going well.

We travelled to Windsor the day before the race. British Blind Sports had arranged for competitors from Norway, Spain, England and Germany to come and compete, and had put us all up in a hotel not far from the park. Race start was not until 1 pm. We woke quite early, ate breakfast, then just relaxed and had a chat about how we wanted to run the race. I had never actually raced that far but was confident I was fit enough to do so and guide as well. We met the others and drove to the park where we collected numbers from the BBS stand and started to get ready.

I had parked the car, and we had gone for a jog in order to get warm; after stretching we wanted to oil groins, underarms and nipples in order to try and stop chaffing, so we needed to get back to the car. There is nothing worse than sweating and getting friction burns, and runners' nipple is nothing short of downright unpleasant. I personally had underestimated the amount of people that were going to be there and had not taken too much notice as to where I had parked the car. It took us way too long to find it and I was getting a little stressed towards the end. We got ready, changed shoes to racing flats and got to the start. The commentator, for want of a better word, had his head screwed firmly on and made a point of stating that there were blind runners in the field: we were connected by rope and that running between us could result in injury to one, both, or all of us. I ran in Day-Glo yellow shorts and vest with the word Guide printed on laminated paper on the back. The gun sounded and we were off.

Because of the amount of training and the weakness in my ankle it was common for the plastic splints in my foot brace to need changing at regular intervals. I had not managed to order any for a while and took it for granted that they would be okay. Nowadays you can get them on a next-day delivery service when ordered online. 'Online' was not even a word back then.

It was warm, reaching around 25°C in the sun, and the course was largely open with little shade available. The drinking stations were regularly placed but they used open-topped soft plastic cups of water. Grabbing one of these when running is hard enough, but Peter was on my right side, meaning he was nearest the drinking stations, and him grabbing a cup had proven nigh on impossible during other shorter races in the lead up to this one.

In order to counter this, we had decided that I would carry a bottle on a belt. The bottle was placed in the small of my back so that it did not interfere with our arm movement. We made a point of drinking regularly; I would reach behind and take the bottle and take a swig myself, then pass it into Peter's right hand. We used verbal commands such as relay runners do at baton change points, and I must say we did well, never dropping the bottle once. When Pete had finished drinking, he would grab the belt just above my hip, and work around to behind me in order to put the bottle back. It meant us having to throttle back slightly but only for a few seconds before we were back at full speed. Someone was at the 8-mile marker with a fresh bottle that was changed as we ran past. It all worked very well.

We had run about 6 miles; we were moving well and if I recall correctly would have been on for a time of around 1 hour and 20 minutes. This is a more than respectable half marathon time by any standard. I could see Terje Løvås a fair way in front of us. He was running really well. At around the 6-mile marker I got a pain high behind the outer ankle bone behind my brace. It didn't really hurt as such but was like having a stone digging in each time, I put my foot down. I thought it was a blister and carried on.

We ran through 10 miles, and according to the split times went through fast in around 1 hour and 2 minutes. This was a record for Peter. He was running fluidly and light on his toes. I felt fine but was getting heavy in the legs. This happens to most people at some stage in a race. They have a bad patch. The cause of this is now seen to be rapid depletion of glycogen levels in the muscles, and nowadays people either train against this or carry electrolyte gels in order to combat this. Everyone knows the bad patch will come. The question usually is when, and for how long.

The section leading to 10 miles was slightly uphill, and I felt it in my thighs almost immediately. For some reason I always struggled running hills, and to an extent still do, although it does not bother me too much now as I do not run anywhere near the pace I did when I was 24. We made a turn and the course flattened out somewhat, my thighs eased, and I hoped I was past the worse of it. Peter showed no signs of fatigue, but he was someone who skied over 12 and 19 miles regularly. We continued and the 12-mile marker came into view.

The Winsor Half Marathon is a tough race. The start and finish are on the same section known as the Long Walk. It is almost a mile long and has a steady incline after around 600 metres. I had thought that this would make things easier approaching the finish, what with it being downhill. The Long Walk is, however, extremely deceptive. From the top, as you start on the long home straight, you can see the finishing post and those who are in front of you. Judging distance in a straight line is hard enough, judging it when you are already physically and mentally tired is a challenge I first encountered then, and still encounter today. The finish never seemed to get any closer. I was starting to struggle; Peter was tiring, and I wanted to get us to the finish as soon as I could. I took control as always and made a slight increase in pace, only to find I had seriously misjudged the distance, and we could not maintain the finishing burst. We crossed the line in just over 1 hour and 21 minutes, a full 2 minutes behind Terje Løvås of Norway.

Peter's strongest nemesis on skis had got the upper hand once again. I was upset. I wanted to beat this guy, just once.

It was not until then that I noticed my ankle was really sore, and Peter noticed that I was limping slightly. On taking off my shoe and foot brace I notice what looked like a lot of blood in my shoe and sock. The splint on the brace had broken and one of the sharp edges had cut into my ankle just behind the bone. We guessed this was what I had felt at 6 miles. I don't think it had an impact on the run; I would have been just as tired at the end. But it does go to show that the endorphins released during running act as a fantastic painkiller, and the renowned runner's high is a wonderful place to be if you are ever there.

We had worked hard for the best part of 6 or more months, with the focus for this one day, this one moment in time. We had come in a little slower than we had both hoped for and anticipated, and we had been beaten once again by Terje. We cooled down, analysed the race, and in essence were satisfied with our performance. We were both tired and decided to take a few days off in order to recover: The Karatethon was looming.

Over the next couple of days, I found it hard to rouse myself into doing anything. I had taken a few days off work and had intended to work more on the Karatethon. I really just could not be bothered though and started thinking again about the race. I was meant to be faster than Peter, yet I had struggled the most. At 10 miles he was more guiding me than me him. Why was this? Had I not been fit enough? We had done the same training, run the same races? Then one thing hit me: it was over, we had worked for a long time towards that one run, and that was it. There we no more competitions for Peter for the next 6 months or more, and, as for me, there were no more individual competitions, ever.

I felt a mixture of elation, the hard training sessions had stopped, and we could go back to doing other things. Yet at the same time I felt immensely guilty, and sad. Had I been the reason Peter was beaten? Was it my fault; and after all that training was that it? I had a chat with

Peter about this over a pint, and he mentioned something called the Big Black Dog. This was a period of depression, that overshadowed an achievement or something good, and which made you look at the positive in a negative light. In running terms, it is now known by another name, 'Post-Race Blues', and it is often those who are first-timers at a long-distance event who struggle the most with it. Not much you can do about it, Peter said, let's get back running. We went out the next day, with very tired legs and a feeling of wondering whether it would ever feel normal again.

THE KARATETHON

It was Sunday morning some weeks later and throughout the areas where Glen had dojos, people were up, bags were packed, and people made their way to Barking for the Karatethon. We were starting at 10 am, and upon entering the hall it was easy to notice the nervous energy and pure excitement in the room. There were around 150 participants up and ready to go. Instructors stood waiting, spectators, of which there were a few, sat waiting, and we began. Twelve hours of karate were about to take place in order to raise as much money as possible in order to help Peter on his way to the Paralympics in Nagano Japan a few years later.

Rules for the day were simple. You trained as little or as much as you wanted. You were sponsored per hour. Each hour was really only 55 minutes, giving everyone the chance to get a drink and a little food during the day. We had been given some fruit and other food by local supermarkets when they closed on the previous day. (Shops were not open 24 hours a day then as they are now.) The training varied from instructor to instructor, hour to hour but after a few hours people began to tire. The children had other rules, which meant they could break mid class and they were not expected to keep going as long as the adults. However, some were really tough and stayed the course pretty much to the end. Others slept for a couple of hours, but everyone wanted to take part in the final hour.

Everyone lined up just before 9 pm. Peter stopped wandering around talking to the parents and those sitting out. His friends, Jimmy Denton and Kenny Bodden, stopped giving their free massages, and my two work colleagues, Jim and Martin, who had been great and taken care of guiding Peter and the others around all day, also sat down. People changed out of their wet gis (karate outfits). They drank, ate and generally got their adrenaline flowing for the last hour. At 9 pm it began.

Glen had decided that he was going to carry out the final Karatethon training alone. The other instructors all took their place in the line. The training was not complicated; people were too tired for that. But it was hard. The final 5 minutes were stationary, punching on the spot and making as much noise as possible. We counted down from 10, and suddenly it was over. I was dead on my feet as was pretty much everyone around me. We had done it. We had planned and pulled off the Karatethon.

Glen remembers more about how it all came about:

> I remember having seen Dave who was one of my students and instructors running one evening when I was on the way to training. I knew he ran but when I saw him running with Pete, I was kind of intrigued. We all went out for a beer after training that night and I got speaking to Dave about this guy he was running with.

> Dave explained about Peter, who he was, what he did, and when he mentioned skiing, I nearly chocked on my beer; when he said it was cross-country skiing, I was even more stunned. This along with the fact that Dave had said Peter was an international and an Olympian blew my mind.

Glen found the fact that Peter was struggling to gain any real solid financial backing somewhat incredible, but it was his wife Julie who came up with a bright idea the next morning.

> We were sitting eating breakfast and Julie just said she had an idea and that we should run a Karatethon over 12 hours to raise money for Pete. We had several little side-lines going at the time plus running the karate club and I thought we had enough on our plates, but she was very persuasive, and I gave Dave a call the same day and we met up. I guess the rest is history.

It was a terrific achievement by everyone who took part and Peter made a rather moving speech saying just that. Not many knew who he was, I don't think many actually even knew why we were raising the money, but the fact that 150 people, plus those helping out, had turned up on a dreary winter's morning in order to try and raise money for him, was something he appreciated, and something he spoke of fondly in the years ahead.

There was only one question left to be answered and that was how much we had managed to collect from sponsors and how far would this take Peter to his dream of a fifth Paralympic Winter Games. The answer to this would have to wait until a few weeks later when the money had been collected, counted and deposited, and the total amount added together. Glen kept this close to his chest and told no one until one Friday late in November 1995 when the presentation party was held in Woodford Green.

THE PRESENTATION

This night was meant to be a celebration of what we had all achieved, and it certainly started in this way. It ended in drunken arguments that made me think about what, if any, future I had within the karate club, or as a guide to Pete.

There was no training that Friday night and people were asked to come for around 7 pm. Glen and Julie had organized some food and the bar that was connected to the dojo was closed for the private party. People arrived and at first were just general mingling and chatting to each other. I had driven Peter who was guest of honour and he was to be presented with a cheque for the yet unknown sponsorship amount.

I was still seeing the young lady from training and had spoken to Peter about her during our runs. We spoke about everything and this was a topic on more than one occasion. I will not divulge details but there was something that I had spoken to him about that had distracted me. Peter being intuitive as he was had picked up on this and had wanted to know what was going on. As mentioned before, Peter always needed to know what was going on, the connection and way we ran was dependent on full disclosure. It was a unique form of intimacy without intimacy, a bond that made us run as well as we did. I told him what I knew, and his reaction was not exactly positive. He told me his thoughts, I decided not to heed his advice, and we carried on as before.

Before the presentation I drove the few minutes down the road to collect my young lady and bring her back for the party. She was jovial and full of energy and came to say hello to Peter. His reaction to her was in my mind somewhat distant and cold but I thought he was just having a harder time than usual orientating himself what with the music and the amount of noise in the room.

Glen called the party to order and made a speech regarding the Karatethon and what had been done. There were a few presentations of small prizes for those that had raised the most money, etc., and we moved onto the finale. The total amount raised at the 12-hour Karatethon was

£10,500!

Everyone in the room did a double take. It was a massive amount of money which far exceeded any expectation we could have imagined. Not everyone had trained the full 12 hours. This amount of money would pay for most of the training trips that Peter needed over the next years in order to train properly for the Paralympics in Nagano. For the first time in the years I had known Peter he was dumbstruck. He stood there opening and closing his mouth like a fish out of water, trying to work out what he should do or say.

After what seemed to be an eternity for me (and most likely for him as well) he smiled and said a very humble thank you to everyone. He said that this was amazing, and that he wished he could thank the club and everyone in it personally, but for now there were two things he could do. First, he wanted to donate £1,500 back to the club in order to subsidize the training and equipment for those that were in a less fortunate position, and second, he wanted to buy everyone there a drink. The latter came from his own pocket.

Glen recalls:

> The amount of money we raised during those 12 hours was nothing short of amazing. There had been a lot of work by those of us in the planning stages, but bottom line is without the 150 or so who met up that Sunday, all the planning in the world would have been useless. It goes to show that in sport, there are no real boundaries. Most of those who met up had never heard of Peter, some never even heard of the Paralympic movement. I think that day a lot of eyes were opened. Would I do it all again for the right cause? Yes, I would without doubt, but the cause would need to be one at least as epic as Peter's was.

Over the course of the evening things got a little hard core on the drinking front. After the smallest children had left, the adults took off somewhat and rounds of drinks were being bought left, right and centre. I was driving so drank no alcohol, but watched Peter get slowly more and more drunk along with some of the others. I had seen it before and knew that the ride home would likely see Peter saying he loved everyone and then he would doze off in the car until I got him home. There were no plans for the Saturday, and we had already agreed to run as normal on Sunday.

I don't like seeing people drunk, I get embarrassed for them and also for the people around them. I felt that Peter was my responsibility that evening and being stone cold sober I decided it was time to get him home. I was on my way back from the toilet and had collected our jackets but could not see or hear Peter. Out of nowhere a friend of mine came and asked me to go with them. Peter had taken certain matters out of my hands and had caused a scene by confronting the young lady I was seeing. To this day I do not know exactly what had happened or what had been said. I do know that Pete had expressed his opinion directly to her and had told her to stop messing with me because I was his friend and he had to look out for me. The young lady stormed off in tears, with me at her heels. She jumped into a taxi and went home, and that was that. Things had finished before they got started. It was the second time that I felt close to someone, only for another person to butt in and tell them to stop playing me around. The other had happened just a few years earlier.

I did nothing more than collect my jacket and leave. I never even thought of how Peter was going to get home and at that point I really did not care. I drove home shaking with anger. I felt let down and betrayed. Worst of all I felt that Peter had been extremely ungrateful and selfish towards the people that had secured his training future for the Nagano Paralympics by giving up a lot of their own time to take part in the event. Not to mention the extra time and effort that Glen, Julie and myself had put in to getting the thing organized.

Saturday arrived and passed, and for the first time in 6 years I did not even think about contacting Peter. I was no longer sure that I even wanted to guide anymore; I felt the trust had gone and that, as we both knew, was a recipe for disaster. We had arranged to run on the Sunday as normal, and despite everything I intended to honour my promise, even if it was for the last time. Peter opened the door when he heard the car as normal but not with his normal happy demeanour. He looked genuinely upset and sad. The normal greeting of 'Hello me son' was replaced with 'Hello Dave'; then he stood and said nothing whilst looking towards the floor.

I said nothing, the awkward silence falling like a rock between us. Peter lifted his head, sucked in air and said: 'Mate, I am sorry. Really I am.' I said nothing; at that point 'Sorry' was not going to cut it. I shuffled my feet and he looked towards me: 'Mate if you are going to clump me, just get it done will you for fucks sake', was the next sentence he spoke to me. I had no intention of hitting him, it would have been a pointless exercise and I would have gained nothing from it.

I told him to get in the car if we were going to run. He did and we drove to Hainault for our Sunday morning run in complete silence, no talking, no music in the car, just the sound of the engine and an atmosphere you could have cut with the proverbial knife.

7

An Uncomfortable Time

We got out of the car, got ready to run and changed shoes all in silence. The rope was already in Pete's hand, as it normally was, for me to pick up when I was ready. I picked the rope up, with a heavy heart. At that particular time, I had absolutely no desire to be there. But there I was, and, seeing as I had come this far, I had to run.

This time it was different though: no small happy chitchat, no discussing how badly West Ham had played and no putting the world to rights as was the norm. Nothing. There was just the steady sound of our feet on the surface of the forest floor and our breathing that was, as always, in sync with each other's. I guided properly; I would not want to do that wrong, and I still had a job to do and intended to do it to the best of my ability as I always did. But that day my heart was not in it. I believed right there and then that this would be our last run, and that on the way home I would tell Pete we were done as a partnership. I felt betrayed; he had broken my trust.

After we had run for a few minutes, I decided that this time I would be calling the shots for once; I was going to steer how far and how fast we went, Pete would just have to hang on. So, I accelerated to a level that I felt Peter was uncomfortable with and maintained that pace. It was normal on our runs that we would throttle back a few times in order not to run too fast. This was something that Peter had taught me to do and something that I do to a certain extent all these years later. However, today this was not going to happen. Today I was going to run out the anger, frustration, adrenaline, disappointment and feeling of betrayal that was inside me. I knew no other way to do it. I would just run and let another more accepted pain take the place of what I was feeling, in the hope it would untie the knot that was wound so tightly inside me.

I felt that we were running much harder than usual after we had run for 4 or 5 miles. We were really moving and, credit to Peter where it was due, he never said a word. Just gritted his teeth, put his head down and ran his heart out. We actually ran extremely well: smooth and fluid, running gentle curves and taking both uphill and obstacles in our stride. Pete was breathing heavily and despite it being cold there was already a deep ring of sweat on his shirt and steam coming from his shoulders.

We continued to run through the grass and mud and all the time I wanted to keep the pace going. I imagine that we ran around 10 or 12 miles that day at a pace that was far faster than we would normally have run. We were not governed by a stopwatch in training. Sometimes we had a rough idea as to how long we had been out, but today was not one of those days.

We got back to the car. I was breathing really heavily and was tired but tried not to bend and rest my hands on my knees. I did not want to give Pete the impression that I too had found the run hard. Pete on the other hand opened the car door and stood in the opening. He leant on the door frame of the car, slightly bent at the shoulders and leant his head on the car. He was sweating profusely and breathing more laboriously than I had ever seen him before.

The he said it, a couple of sentences that broke the atmosphere in an instant and made us both laughs. 'Oh God, you nasty little fucker', 'You dir-r-t-y-bastard', followed by a wretch as he vomited onto the floor by the car. It came from nowhere and the tension eased considerably almost at once. We changed and jogged a little to shake the lactic acid that was clearly building up in both of us, got in the car and I drove back. This time there was still nothing other than a little chitchat, but the radio was on at least. There was nothing mentioned about what had happened on Friday, and I never told him that we had run our last run. My head was full of confusing thoughts. Over the day

I came to a decision. I would continue to guide; of course, I would. We had argued once in 6 years, and despite the nature, severity and cause of the argument, I would not just dump Pete. It didn't work like that. I didn't work like that. Pete and I didn't work like that. We had been a partnership for 6 years. There was no reason to stop that now. The incident was never mentioned again. Pete was obviously only trying to protect me in his own way, and time is a great healer after all.

Our training continued in the same manner as it had always done, but things were still somewhat strained between us for a while. Joan and Sid, Pete's parents and it was noticed a couple of times when I dropped Peter off; I either didn't go for a cuppa, or, if I did, the normal friendly jokey banter was just not there. I don't know whether Peter ever told his parents what had happened or why, but they never tried to defend him to me, and, as far as I recall, they never pried into why the atmosphere had suddenly changed. I guess they thought we were two grown men, who should be able to iron out their differences on their own.

Throughout this time Peter had still not had any time on snow. The snow was not deep enough to set tracks in Hønefoss where his guide Dag lived, and his other guide, Lyder, was for some or other reason not available to help out. The snow had still not arrived in Beitostølen and there were events coming up in the middle part of March. Pete became pretty despondent, knowing that without snow time there was no way for him to tune his technique. It had been almost 8 months since he had stood on skis, and I was not competent enough to make corrections on the static Nordic ski machine that he had in the training room. We made up for it by mixing sessions up, and training with John on the track. We picked up as many races as we could in the hope these would at least bring some race fitness to Pete that he could transfer over to the skis when the snow eventually arrived. The transition from road to snow is not easy. Different muscles are used in different ways so the only thing we could get really fit were his lungs.

It was after Christmas; the atmosphere was lighter between us, but it was nowhere near the same as it had been before that fate-filled evening earlier in the winter. We were in a monotonous routine which did not make things easier, and Pete was naturally enough becoming more and more frustrated with there still being no snow. He had friends living and working in Beitostølen and they promised to update him and give word as soon as the snow came, and tracks were cut.

Late one Monday afternoon, in mid-January 1996, my office telephone rang. It was Pete. He sounded both a little apprehensive and excited and told me he had just received word that it had 'snowed like a bastard in Beitostølen'. He had already asked his two Norwegian guides to come for a week's training, but it was too short notice for them, and they could not make it. He asked if I had any possibility of getting the time off. He had already reserved two tickets from London to Oslo for the following Wednesday, 2 days later, but needed to confirm them in the next half an hour or so. My boss was at her desk and after a brief discussion said she had no issue with me taking a week off even though it was short notice. People were extremely understanding and sympathetic to the cause. Peter and I were often seen by my work colleagues running past their cars whilst they sat in traffic jams on their way home from work, and he was quite the local celebrity in Barking and Dagenham. I rang Pete back and he confirmed the tickets.

We trained as usual that evening, the atmosphere a lot lighter than it had been for a long time. There were things to discuss about our trip, about what training targets we had for the week we had available, and how on earth was I going to guide him on skis when I had only been on them once. Eventually, the question arose regarding money and accommodation. Pete had not exactly managed to find a hotel for us to stay in yet but had friends in Beitostølen working on this. My bank card would not work abroad, I had no traveller's cheques to use and it was too late to order Norwegian Kroner and get them delivered in time for our trip. Peter's answer was simple. This was a necessary training trip, he needed me there in every sense of the word as he could not do it on his own. This meant that in his mind it was something that he would pay for using the sponsor money raised through the Karatethon.

We were up early Wednesday; the flight was the same as ever at 10.20 am. From experience we knew that we would need to allow extra time for checking in Peter's skis, and he was nearly always stopped at security control. This was mainly due to him always taking his tuning tools in his hand baggage, so he could have a look over the pianos at the Bergo and Bitihorn hotels. In return his bar bill was always a little lighter at the end of the week than maybe it would have been otherwise.

I collected Pete at just after 5 am and, as always, we drove the extra 15 minutes to his parents' house. His mum was waiting as she always did with a couple of lunch boxes, a kiss and hug for us both, and wishes of a good and safe journey. From there we made the journey through London to Heathrow, parked and got to the check-in desk. It was going to be a long day; we had eaten the sandwiches so headed to one of the restaurants for breakfast, where we discussed the training plan for the week ahead.

Peter had spoken the previous evening to Dag who had seen me on skis in Beitostølen during the Ridderrennet the previous April and confirmed to Pete that over a longer distance I was not good enough to keep up with him, let alone guide him. But, seeing as we would be using the tracks at Helsesportssenteret (basically an arena used for rehabilitation of sports injuries) we could ski some 2- and 3-minute intervals. The tracks were pretty much flat and there were long straights that we could use. Dag was sure that this would be a perfect set up, and, in addition, he had managed to get some time off towards the end of the week and would make the drive-in order to train with Pete at least for the weekend. Peter had just turned 40 and Dag had arranged for a surprise party as well, unbeknown to us.

I must admit I was a little apprehensive at the thought that I, who had only ever been on skis for 7 days, would be trying to guide someone like Peter who had been competing internationally since 1976, when I was only 5 years old. I really didn't hold much faith in my ability for this undertaking, so took one of Dad's refereeing whistles, thinking that I could at least signal to Peter when the interval was over. As normal we went to the bar to wait, but this time I also had a beer as we waited for the flight to be called.

Arriving at Oslo Fornebu was different this time. There were still lots of people, but we needed to get to the central bus terminal and find the right bus going to Valdres, and then drive through Geilo to Beitostølen. It was only the second time I had seen the Norwegian language written and had no idea as to how these words should be pronounced. Pete was trying his best by spelling the words but things like 'an O with a line and some dots or something' meant nothing to me. (For info, he was referring to the letter Ø which is one of the three extra letters in the Norwegian alphabet that are not in the English alphabet.) The other alternative was to hire a car and drive. It was snowy, and I had never driven on the right side of the road before (i.e. the wrong side if you are English), so we decided against it.

In the end, someone at the bus station helped us and showed us to the bus. It was smaller than I remembered but was empty. The headphones went on and I dozed a while, all the time wondering how on earth it could be so dark so early. It was only around 2 pm. The bus jolted to a stop and braked hard. Looking out of my window I saw the cause standing to the left side of the road a few metres in front of the bus: a moose. I had never seen one before and was somewhat awed by the size of it. I found out afterwards that moose are the cause of many car incidents in Norway during the course of a year. As a rule, an 800-kilogram lump of sold muscle hitting a car tends to not end well for either parties involved.

We arrived at Beitostølen later in the evening than we had before. I don't remember the exact time, but I would imagine it must have been around 7.30 pm, or maybe even later. As we got off the bus one of Peter's friends, Kjell Arne, was waiting. He was the bartender at the Bergo Hotel and had managed to find us accommodation in the staff quarters. It was nothing fancy, but Peter and I needed a bed and a shower, that was all. Food was to be had at the Bergo. There was someone else standing not far away, a girl with medium-long blonde hair. The same girl I had met in April who had dropped the glasses. She had just arrived to start her seasonal work in the area, as she had done for many years. I would make a point to try and talk to her this time around.

The accommodation was very basic. There was no space for the skis indoors and no ski room, so we stood them outside. We could keep the wax warm and Pete knew what to do here. Bags were stuffed at the end of the beds and we hung up a couple of pairs of trousers and some shirts to drop out the creases; the rest stayed in the bag. We headed to the restaurant in the hotel. Serving time had finished a long time ago and the room was empty, but Kjell Arne had spoken with the cook who had managed to find some leftovers and warm them up for us. The meat was tender in a thick creamy brown sauce. I had never tasted anything like it. It turned out that this was the second encounter I had had with a moose on the same day.

We were both tired, so it was an early night that night. We set the alarm and woke early in order to get breakfast in good time before training. We both liked having a couple of hours after eating before training and made a point of eating well at the pre-training meal. The hotel was around 600 metres from the accommodation block, so naturally we walked. It was still dark, with just some faint light from the streetlamps; the air was cold, and fresh and the snow crisp and crunchy underfoot. During the short walk my nose and face started to go numb, and as we walked past the thermometer mounted on the wall of a building, I realized why: it was just after 7 am, and it was minus 30°C. I had never experienced cold like it.

We started training around 10 that morning. Pete waxed the skis outside our accommodation, and we walked the mile or so to Helsesportssenteret where we going to train. Pete got his skis on in seconds, but I struggled with the bindings and it took me ages. We went for a gentle couple of miles skiing to warm up. I was like Bambi on ice, only worse. I was all over the place and had no co-ordination.

The lack of co-ordination was really rather strange though; the cross-country skiing technique is not that different from running, with the left arm forward when the right leg is forward. The only difference is that you slide the leg forward pulling from the hip rather than lifting the leg. There is still the transfer of weight from one side to the other and there is still the kick phase on the back leg in order to move forwards. It took a little while, Peter being patient and trying to ski next to me in order to watch as he called it.

After a while I got the hang of it, but it was going to be a long week if this was the way things were going to be. After the warmup we started the training. I noted we were doing timed intervals around the arena. This was great for me. It meant that I could either ski with Pete, or if I could not keep up with him, as I suspected might be the case, I could nip across to another point whilst still being able to see him all the time. We were skiing 2-minute intervals, with a short 45-second break. I was fine for the first couple and skied with the whistle in my mouth in case Pete left me standing. After a few intervals it was clear I was not going to be much help anymore. I was falling badly behind early on, although hanging on as best as I could. Peter was going hell for leather as always and had no one in front or beside him to warn him of any obstacles. I was worried he was going to hit something.

The first repetition without me was okay. I could see him all the way through, and the whistle was loud enough for him to hear. He lost a little momentum around one of the bends but had done that when I was with him anyway. The speed he was moving at was absolutely stunning. There were other sighted skiers warming up nearby and they looked on with amazement.

Towards the end of the last Interval I checked the watch and counted down to the finish. I blew on the whistle, but it was still well below freezing and the pea had frozen. Pete kept using double tuck and as he came past, I had to shout at him to stop. He stopped, cocked his head and smiled at me, muttering one of his endearing expletives as was his nature. We walked back, changed out of some extremely sweaty clothes, and got ready for lunch.

Back then there was little known about sports nutrition and fuelling for sport. Pete's thinking was simple: we burn so many calories doing this that we have to feed the beast. So, we did. We sat and went through soup and a main course at lunch; it was a buffet so there was more than one serving. We went back to the room, found clean clothes, changed, and looked forward to the afternoon session.

That week we pretty much followed this schedule, until around Thursday. Dag arrived and decided we should go on a long ski for stamina purposes. This would be long: likely 30 or more kilometres. Both Pete and Dag thought me being with them would be good. It would mean they kept the pace down. It would be a day off for me with no guiding and would give me more of an insight as to how they did their bit. I would also be able to see if I could adopt anything they did and adapt it to running. In addition, it meant I got to ski, behind them, without worrying about trying to pace Peter. Like that was ever going to happen!

We started off at Helsesportssenteret, nice and easy as was the plan. Dag knew a route that would take us away from the arena and up into the mountains. Pete and he were fantastic to watch on skis. Dag guiding in a mixture of Norwegian and English and Pete following as he always did. I was hanging on at the back, something that Pete noted, and he called for a time out. I must have been a good 30 seconds behind them and had just stopped in order to get some water when they were off again. It continued this way for a good couple of hours, until in the end I shouted for them to wait. The response was, in hindsight, hysterical. Pete came to an instant halt and called for Dag to stop. Dag stopped, looking confused and wondering what was wrong, and Peter telling him: 'Shit! Dag! Fucking Dave is still hanging on the poor bastard.'

You could almost hear the sharp intake of breath. I caught up with them after about a minute I guess and leaned against my ski poles trying to get my breath. I am not exactly sure how I ended up skiing down the road alone back towards the resort centre. I vaguely remember being pointed in that direction by Dag and being told to take that path, whilst he and Peter skied the rest of the route. My route back was not without its own small incidents either, truth be known, but I got to the accommodation and sat on the bed waiting for Pete and Dag to arrive. They woke me an hour later, still in my ski gear in a heap on the bed.

We ate again, but this time there were three of us and the buffet was demolished. I guess we ate constantly for the best part of 45 minutes, before all going back to our room and relaxing. I was reading a book of some sort and had connected the Walkman to portable speakers so that we had some music. We agreed that my day of skiing was finished, and Pete and Dag went out alone. I fully intended to read my book but woke when Pete and Dag returned a while later, still on the same page, book lying over my face.

Over the remaining days Dag took me out for some one-on-one ski training. He was more than competent as most Norwegians are, and he seemed to confirm the adage that Norwegians are born with skis on their feet. In the course of those few hours with him, my technique improved massively, and although I was never going to be able to guide Pete in races, I was going to be able to help him train on other occasions.

On the Friday evening with the help of many of Peter's friends in Beitostølen a party was held in order to celebrate his 40th birthday. Peter was held in much affection in Beitostølen amongst those who knew him, in the same manner as he was pretty much everywhere. It was great evening, with lots of good food and enough drink to go around. Some people who had not been officially invited turned up anyway as is always the case; including the girl with the medium-long blonde hair who I had seen on more than one occasion. I found out her

144

name was Marit. Over the course of the evening we spoke a lot about nothing in particular, and although there was never any holiday romance this time either I did come away with her home telephone number. I understood she was studying at the time and would be returning to Oslo a week or so later but would perhaps be returning to Beitostølen for the Ridderrennet in April.

Things between me and Peter were now back to how they always had been. The break in Norway had been good in many ways. It had relieved his frustration that he was not getting snow time. It had shown me that he really was only ever looking after my interests, regardless of whether or not I agreed with him at the time. I had also established a good relationship with Dag, and he had explained to me in detail what he wanted us to focus on for the future.

Initially I was not going to go to Beitostølen in 1996, despite my name being put down. I had injured the ankle again, and the father of a friend of mine, Maurice Bull, had stepped in to take some runs with Peter. However, I recovered enough to feel that even if I could not ski that much, I was still going to be able to help the group as a whole; and the atmosphere within the group and the after-ski at Svingen pub with Kenny Bodden drunk and singing was worth the trip on its own. The night before we travelled, I found my passport and other stuff I might need and came across a piece of paper with the name Marit and a telephone number on it. A number I had not looked at, let alone called, since we had come home in January the same year. So, I screwed it up, and threw it away, thinking that I would never see her again anyway. We travelled to Norway, got off the bus in Beitostølen and there, waiting at the bus stop with Kjell Arne, was the girl with the medium-long blonde hair: Marit.

Over the course of the week the snow conditions deteriorated drastically making the snow wet. Skiing was limited to certain times of the day and those who were neither guiding nor competing were politely asked not to use the tracks so they would be in at least adequate condition for the races ahead. Instead I got to see a bit of the area. Marit had arranged to borrow a car and take me on a sightseeing tour. When she collected me there was another girl in the car who was coming along for the ride; I believe her name was Lene and she worked with Marit at the Bergo.

The ski festival went as normal. Pete was competing hard by day and partying hard at night, along with Kenny and the others. After the last day of racing on the Saturday, the boys really took off. They had brought with them their quota of duty free and decided to have a hotel room party for those that wanted to come. Basically, this meant that people bought their own glasses and all the drinks were collected onto a table where people helped themselves. I imagine this started at about 3 pm and with dinner not before 6 in the evening there were a few people worse for wear as we reached the dining room. They were good-humoured though and were not over boisterous or rowdy. But I have never before seen prawns eaten without being peeled, in such amounts. In all, it was just a little embarrassing. At dinner no one drank anything other than water. (Norwegian water is very good. Most towns and cities stopped using chlorine to clean the water many years ago, preferring to use ozone and ultraviolet radiation to sterilize it instead. The result is water that is clean, crisp and almost sweet tasting.) The only other water that was drunk that night was tonic water topped up with copious amounts of gin.

Towards the end of the evening I bumped into Marit who was just finishing her shift. It was late, and we were to travel very early the next day. I got her home phone number again, and her parents address, and promised I would write. Then I set about trying to find Pete and get him back to the room so he could pack. I couldn't find him, and no one had seen him for a while since he had left with a young lady. I headed back to the room.

There was an unwritten rule in the group of singles that if there was a room key showing on the outside of the door, the room was occupied, and it was not appropriate for anyone to enter. As I came to our room, I saw no key, so opened the door and walked in; then turned

146

promptly and walked out again rather quickly. Obviously, Pete and his new friend had forgotten the rule.

Pete came down to the bar a while later, as though nothing had ever happened. It was getting really late, and my concern was how on earth people would make the bus the next morning. I decided that I at least needed to be awake enough to help out so went to bed. Pete was still fully dressed when I woke the next morning and I never actually found out whether he had ever gone to bed in order to sleep the evening before. There was, however, a strong smell of gin and alcohol about him. The room on the other hand showed no real signs of the party the previous evening. We boarded the bus at about 7.30 am and most of the guys were asleep before we left the car park. They were all a little groggy when we arrived at Fornebu for our flight home. We managed to check in without incident and got to our plane. Again, they were asleep before we took off. It had obviously been a hard day's night for them. Since then I have never been back to Beitostølen other than when driving through on the way to somewhere else. This is something that I hope to rectify at some stage in the future.

We were now at the end of the winter season of 1996 and began to look forward at how we were going to deal with the summer season. I was not racing for myself anymore after 'retiring' the previous summer, but we needed to do something. We signed up once more for the Windsor Half Marathon, to be held in September 1996, and John was once again on hand to set the training. We had 6 months of hard work ahead plus races. But Peter had another idea. He wanted to run some 400-metre races to see just how fast he could run. Pete was someone who was not scared. He did not care whether he won, drew or lost. He was not built for speed. He was extremely strong and had massive stamina, but his leg speed was maybe a little less suited to the long sprints.

Pete's previous best time was around 62 seconds but that had been run before my time. Halfway through May 1996 Peter suffered a slight setback. Whilst training he tore a calf muscle high into the

147

gastrocnemius. It was not a bad tear, but it was in the transition between the gastrocnemius and soleus muscles and sat deep. He rested and after a week was symptom free, so we ventured a short run on grass. He stretched out to try a short stride, then pulled up. It was back. This time it was slightly worse than before. It was time for an enforced break, and trips to the physio, Geoff Mimms.

Pete knew Geoff from way back, and it had been Geoff who had kept me going when I suffered from the ankle injury that had stopped me competing. He was a gentle but an extremely good physiotherapist, and he saw Peter a couple of times a week for about a fortnight. In addition, he gave Pete clear instructions as to what he should and should not do. After two weeks of treatment Pete's muscle tear was much better, and we gingerly set out on a training run, building up slowly; by late June we were back in full flight.

The training was going well. Pete had no sign of his injury and, although we never trained specifically for a 400-metre race, Pete really wanted to try one, just to see how far off his best of 62 seconds he was. Even though I had stopped training for myself and had stopped racing, I was still faster than he was. My own best was just around the 50-second mark, so I had capacity to run sub 60 with him. When I was competing, the first lap of an 800-metre race would have been somewhere around the 53–55-second mark.

We entered an open event at Woodford Green Athletics track in late August 1996. These open events were vital if people were going to be race fit at the right time and they held probably one a month from April through to the end of the season. The way it worked was that the runner put down the time they predicted they would finish. The arrangers would then seed the races so that athletes of around the same standard would be grouped together. This meant that, first, races were going to be competitive without a runaway winner; and, second, that you could put a time down slightly faster than you had run before, in order to try and force a new Personal Best out of yourself.

We registered, explaining that Peter was blind and that we would need to run two in the same lane. I asked Peter what time he wanted to put down for seeding. He said 60 seconds, which was 2 seconds inside his best. I wrote 58 ensuring he was going to be in a fast race.

During the warm up we came up with a very simple strategy: start as hard as we could; run as fast as possible down the back straight and into the final bend and use the bend's momentum to push us into the final 100 metres; lift the knees and then hang on for dear life and hope we had gone fast enough. This time it was my territory and Pete gave me free control from start to finish. The only condition we had to abide to, in keeping with the rules governing blind athletics, was that the athlete must cross the line first not the guide. After all it was his time that counted, not mine.

I recall we were drawn on one of the inside lanes, which made the turns sharper than we would have liked. I could hear the slight sniggers from the side-line as Peter and I prepared and took a few final strides. You could almost hear the doubt and amusement in people's voices. Was a blind man going to run in a fully able-bodied sprint race? Or were these two men holding hands? We took our marks, and everyone went into their normal sprint start, but not Peter and me.

I remember the race vividly, maybe because it was the first time, we had ever raced on the track together in an able-bodied event, or maybe it was just that the entire experience burned itself into my memory. The gun went and the race was on. I ran hard, the rope smooth between us, not snapping, meaning that Pete and I were in sync with each other; after the initial 2 or so metres Pete was in total sync, stride for stride. We had run bends a lot and Pete leaned in his full weight onto me; it was tricky, as there are a lot of forces in motion when two men with a combined weight of nearly 20 stone lean to one side at speed.

There was a lot of pressure on my legs and my own mind wandered slightly; I was hoping that the ankle would hold up under the pressure despite being in its brace. It did. There were no verbal commands now, other than giving him a short update on how far was left to go. We came off the first bend having already eaten into the stagger on the lanes outside of us. Quite unexpectedly, I felt two short tugs on the rope: Pete wanted to go faster. So, we opened our stride as one unit and the back straight went past surprisingly quick. As we hit the 200-metre mark I hit the lap button on my watch to check later.

As we came off the last bend, we were in third place. It was neck and neck and, although he was tiring badly and treading water, Pete was still strong. We edged in front over the last 10 metres and won in a time of around 58.5 seconds. He had broken his best by 3 seconds at the age of 40, and some 12 years after he had set it.

The split showed the first 200 to be around 27, a second best in the same race. The other runners came to congratulate us; there were no more sniggers and comments that day, more nods of admiration, and I felt so proud. Finally, there was an acceptance that disabled athletes should be seen as real competitors in races. Pete had after all just beaten seven other able-bodied runners.

Pete was a humble man. If he won on the day, he would say he had a good day; if he lost, the others were better than him, there were no excuses. As long as he could walk away and say that he did the best he could, at that given point in time, then no one could say anything against that. This attitude has been somewhat lacking in recent years, but in blind sports, particularly, the competitors were not sponsored: they worked, and they were then, and remain, amateurs in every sense of the word. Once again Peter had proven that disabled or not, he was more than a match for many on any given day. I believe that this was without doubt our best race, and I also believe that the fact we had not taken part in the 1992 Summer Paralympic Games was a big mistake.

I had written to Marit after our time spent in Beitostølen, nothing major, just general chitchat, and had heard nothing I return. I decided to make one more effort, and then that was it. I was not going to chase anymore, there were other fish in the sea. I received a letter mid-June from her saying she was coming over to London and wondered if she could stay. My parents were okay with it, but it was not until I called to speak with her that I found out she would be arriving the next day. Over the course of the next months I travelled to Norway to visit her and planned a trip in September after she had started her degree course at the University of Stavanger. On returning from this trip I had decided that I was going to take a chance and move. The move was planned for June 1997 but not without long discussions with Peter. He had Nagano in March of 1998 and would not go if he did not have a guide who could help him train for it. That was not fair on him.

In the meantime, however, there was a lot that could happen and stop a move planned for nearly a year ahead, so we never really paid that much attention to it. We did have the Windsor Half Marathon to contend with again and based on the year before we knew there were areas we needed to focus on. We dropped one of the track sessions a week and added a second-long run. Now our training week was 6 days: there was one day of short intervals, one day of long intervals, two long-run days with hill climbs incorporated into one of them, and two days that were more recovery based but rarely under 8 miles. I guess we ran 40 or so miles on the runs outside of intervals and it seemed to be doing us good. We entered various distance races from 5 miles and upwards. We felt strong and were moving well. Things were looking good.

Marit was over at the time of the Windsor Half Marathon in September. Peter had already decided that he wanted to travel up on the morning of the race, as there was less temptation to have a beer or two with the others at the hotel. We arrived in good time, warmed up well and were really looking forward to the race. We started well, Peter controlling the speed as normal and me working on trying to find the easiest route for us to run. The race was now very popular and there were over 2,000 runners in place. The Long Walk is rather narrow, not more than about 9- or 10-feet wide at best. With this number of people, it was important for us to run as unhindered as possible and preferably without breaking stride pattern too often. We were slow at the first mile – there were too many people – but after the first mile surge was over, space opened, and we could run freely. We had not got too far when Pete slowed drastically. There was no prior warning, and he was not limping. He told me he had got stitch of all things, right under his ribcage.

For those that have had it you will know that having the stitch is debilitating. It hurts to move, and it hurts to breath. After the worst was past, we increased speed again. It stayed with him for a few miles and then was gone, just as fast and just as mysteriously as it had arrived. We had lost time by now, but carried on running regardless, passing 10 miles about a minute or so outside our time from the year before.

There was nothing we could do about it, so we carried on running, increasing our speed over the last 2 miles and passing as many runners as we could. We finished only 30 seconds or so slower than the year before and were pleased; had the stitch not been there we may well have broken the 1 hour 21-minute mark that we wanted. Still there was always next year.

During that winter of 1996, it was time to make sure that Peter had a guide or guides to take my place when I moved away. Pete contacted Maurice Bull again and arranged that they would run, with me following to give any pointers that might be needed. This felt strange; Pete and I had established our own system, but then maybe the mental bond or whatever it was we shared was the instigator here. He also found someone from the Metro club, whom he could use for track sessions. Things had worked themselves out and on 26 June 1997 I ran my last regular run with Pete and said a tearful farewell to him, Sid and Joan. I moved to Norway the day after, and for a while felt as though I had lost a limb; something was missing. I spoke with Peter on a daily basis. The one thing I did do was to carry on running. I wanted to be in shape to run with Peter at every opportunity I could.

THE END OF AN ERA

From the time I moved in 1997 things got hard for Peter. Not in the way of training; he had John and those at the track always willing to step in and take a session with him, and at least one person who was willing to do longer runs with him. But, on a personal front the next 6 months were extremely hard.

I had been in Norway for about a month. I still had no employment other than seasonal work, and my funds were dwindling fast. We were basically living in student accommodation and existing on Marit's student loan. The telephone rang one afternoon. It was Dawn, Pete's girlfriend of the time. She said that Joan, Pete's mum, had died of a heart attack, suddenly and without warning, and that Pete needed me home. He wanted to know when I could travel and would make the arrangements. The centre of Pete's world had been taken from him; he needed me and there was never any question as to whether or not I was going. I was on the first available plane back to London.

I stayed in England for 10 days or so in order to be there for the funeral and just to be around Peter. Pete and I ran as we had always done, but more for therapeutic reasons than training. Running gave Pete an escape from his own mind, gave him something to think about; he ran hard. He was angry and couldn't understand why Joan had been taken from him so abruptly? One half of the pair of family kingpins was gone; she had been his rock, always. After one run Peter wanted to talk, so we talked, and I think for the first and last time ever I saw Peter cry. Great shuddering but tearless sobs rocked through him and all I could do was be there, hold him, support him and hope that his pain would pass and that he would get back on an even keel. Pete was broken and I had no idea as to how I could fix him. He was vulnerable; the larger than life Pete that I knew so well and loved so much, whom I had shared so much of my life with over that last decade, withered in front of me. I felt powerless with him for the first time. The funeral was a smallish affair. Pete sat there, silent throughout the entire service and said nothing. Our daily contact continued after I returned to Norway, and Pete appeared to be returning to his normal self.

Pete continued his training. We had already registered for the '97 Windsor Half Marathon before I moved to Norway and much of the work, we had done in the preceding years was still in the system, needing nothing more than topping up. I was in good shape having been running during the day whilst in Stavanger and I was optimistic that we could do well. The race was in late September, almost exactly 2 months after his mum had passed away.

As in the previous year, Pete did not want to go to the hotel the night before. He said he wanted to run the race, but even in the warmup it was clear there was something wrong. I knew it, and so did he. He had no spring in his step; was generally flat and appeared to have no energy. His warmup was very short, and he never broke into a sweat. We lined up. Pete was not his happy self this time but sucking in deep lungsful of air and releasing them as big sighs. The gun went, and we started. He was lethargic and unresponsive to my signals on the rope trying to get some spring in his step. It felt like we were crawling along. The rope was snapping between us as we were out of sync, and for the first time I wondered if the Black Dog that had visited him in 1984, causing him to pull out of the Olympics, was making a return. With his mum only dying a few short months before, he would have had every right not to run, every reason to pull to the side, and I would have both understood this and supported him fully. His mind was not in the game, and he was going through the motions. He appeared disinterested.

We got to about halfway, we were running easily, and I tried again to pick up the pace a little. Pete was never one to race halfway, either he ran his heart out, or he never bothered, such was his nature. A fighter from the day he was born. There was no reason for him to stop now. This time the response was there. He appeared to snap out of whatever trance he was in. The pace quickened and we were once again running smoothly as one unit, passing people, but not being passed.

We ran through the 10-mile marker some way off where we had been two years before. I think we were around the 65-minute mark. Pete had his head in the game and pushed on. My fear was that we would pay for the increase in pace during the last 5 kilometres, but this did not happen. He ran superbly, the last 5 kilometres in just around 18 minutes, and including a full sprint at the end. We were slower than the years before yes, but not by much. It seemed the race did Pete good. It snapped him out of his building depression and got his focus back on Nagano the following March. This would be Peter's final Olympics; he wanted to do his absolute best and was well on the way to achieving this.

About a month later I got a call from Pete's girlfriend again, this time saying that Peter had been involved in an accident. He had been run over on a pedestrian crossing in the dusk of a wet, foggy November evening. The pedestrian crossing was the one he always used, not more than 100 metres or so from his home. The damage was not yet known, but there was a suspicion of a broken leg. Later the same evening it was confirmed. Pete had a lot of soft tissue damage and the leg was swollen; there was a break in the tibia, just below the knee. Luckily it was not that bad, and the doctors praised Peter's muscular fitness as a factor that likely stopped the damage being worse. He was in plaster for 4 weeks but continued to train with ski-related upper-body exercises, and after 4 weeks he was back in business pushing towards the 1998 Winter Paralympics.

The Nagano Olympics were in March 1998. It was the first trip to Japan for the entire team and people really did not know what to expect. It was a long journey. Pete had trained to the best of his considerable ability from December onwards and hoped that he would maybe be able to compete in the shorter distances. He had missed too much mileage and snow time to be a threat in the longer distances but was going to give it his best shot. He was never one to turn up just to make up the numbers.

Once again, the two Norwegians and the Russians were too strong, and Pete came home from Nagano empty handed. His best placement being fourth in the 5-kilometre biathlon race. He was not bitter, he had given his all, but his Paralympic career spanning 24 years and 7 games was over. He had travelled to places many of us only dream of, he had competed at a level most never reach, and he had won medals at all levels in three sports, from European Championships to Olympic medals. He possessed a dogged determination that makes the difference between being a competitor and a challenger. A determination that many, I included, wished they possessed, but which only a few ever managed to have. In later years I wondered how good Peter would have been had he been a sighted runner without the restraints imposed by his blindness; someone who could run and train when they wanted and without his dependency on others. He was not finished internationally, though, and would continue to compete, or at least that was the plan.

8

MORE AWARDS

Reflecting upon the Nagano Paralympics and the fact that even with less than optimal training he had still managed to finish fourth in one event, Peter remained optimistic that maybe, all things being well, he could set yet another record and attend his eighth Winter Games in Salt Lake City in 2002.

This would mark almost 20 years since his first European gold in 1983 and 30 years since his international debut in Austria in 1974. He was further motivated by being awarded the Pery Medal by the Ski Club of Great Britain in 1999.

The Pery Medal is awarded by the Council of the Ski Club of Great Britain to a skier, individual or organization for an outstanding contribution to snowsports, and was instituted in 1929 by the Hon. E. C. Pery, later the Earl of Limerick, DSO and President of the Ski Club of Great Britain (1925–1927).

In order to be recognized by the Council the nominee must have made a notable contribution to the knowledge of mountaincraft in relation to skiing, achieved distinction in exploration on skis, notably advanced the technique of skiing, made an outstanding contribution to the success of competitive international skiing, or made an outstanding contribution to the development of snowsports.

Peter had met several of these criteria with his contribution to the development of snowsports for the visually impaired and also having made an outstanding contribution. He was, after all, a visually impaired winter sports competitor who had gained more international recognition and championship medals than any of his sighted counterparts.

At that time, in 1999, Peter was the first and only visually impaired athlete to have been recognized by the Ski club of Great Britain and remained so until the medal was also awarded to Kelly Gallagher and Jade Etherington and their guides Charlotte Evans and Caroline Powell, after the 2014 Paralympics in Sochi.

The award in 1999 was ground-breaking. It was widely publicized and opened the way for further sponsorship for British blind winter sports; and with Peter as its ambassador, things gained momentum and looked brighter.

The year 1999 also saw the birth of my first daughter, and naturally I wanted Peter to be part of her life as well as mine. With this in mind I asked him to be godfather to Sara. He accepted without a second thought, but because of other commitments he was unable to attend the christening in Norway in February 2000. Fortunately, we had also arranged for a blessing to be held for Sara in my local parish church back in England and this time, in Dagenham at Easter 2000, Peter was there. He had never struck me as a God-fearing man, although in my heart I do believe that he had at least a little faith.

He attended the service and sang the best he could. Hymn books were obviously not available in Braille, but amazingly enough he knew most of the hymns that were sung. When he did not know the words of the hymn, he hummed along, adding the word 'watermelon' or 'apricot' at various points so at least it seemed that he knew what he was singing.

The service neared the end and we were asked to pray. As Peter knelt in front of the church bench, the stillness of the church was disturbed by the sound of ripping cloth. It had been a number of years since Peter had worn a suit and the leg seams on his trousers had torn. He gritted his teeth until he came out of the church and then released a few choice words that would not have been suitable inside.

Peter and I still had the most fantastic connection despite the fact that I was living away; it was still so natural and, as was always the case when I visited home, we arranged to run the next day. After the run in which nothing untoward or unusual happened I noted a small lump on the calf of Peter's leg. It is not unusual to burst a small blood vessel in the calf when training, as there is a great amount of pressure on this particular muscle through the drive and push off phase of the running movement, but I mentioned it to Peter. He said it had been there a little while and was a little sore when he knocked it, but it would pass.

ANOTHER SETBACK

After Easter that year, I didn't travel back to London again until near the end of August. Pete was once again struggling to get a guide but was managing to maintain his training in the training room he had in the garden. The lump on his leg, however, was larger, a lot larger now, around the size of a chicken's egg. It was sore to the touch, hindered his training and rubbed on his clothes; after much persuasion by me and his family, Peter went to his doctor and was referred to a specialist at the local hospital. He was waiting to be called in for his appointment, but he still did not seem particularly bothered. However, he limped slightly when he ran, and it was obvious he was not at all comfortable.

I travelled back to Norway but was also waiting anxiously for his appointment to come through. Although Peter did not appear outwardly too concerned, I knew that this was not really the case. It was not until Christmas 2000 that I travelled back to be with my family, and once again to run with Peter. Peter's leg was too sore to run, and the mass was now considerably larger than it had been a few short months earlier. There was still no confirmation from the hospital in regard to an appointment and it was noticeable that Peter was starting to get really worried. I am not medically trained in any way, but a mass that increases from the size of a pea to the size of a large plum in such as short space of time was indeed something that started the alarm bells ringing.

He contacted his GP and obtained an appointment a short while after Christmas, at the beginning of 2001. As far as we knew, the mass had been there for nearly a year and yet there had still been no form of contact with the hospital. Peter's GP was concerned enough to tell Peter to forget about the referral to the hospital and instead to go directly to the Accident and Emergency unit, which he did, and a tissue biopsy was planned.

I am not entirely sure of the chronological correctness of events here, but I seem to remember that it was sometime prior to Peter having the biopsy and getting his results that fate dealt another cruel hand in his life. I was at home in Norway when I received a call telling me that Peter's father Sid had died. It was all quite sudden, and I only found out later that he had died of lung cancer. The second kingpin in the Young family unit was gone. Pete was knocked for six as can be expected and once more I travelled back to the UK in order to try and be there as support for Peter. Besides, I had known Sid for many years.

Pete was much the same at this funeral as he had been at his mum Joan's a few years earlier. He said very little, but, as people gathered around the mass of flowers that were outside the crematorium, he made the quip that there was always one more funeral to go to. It was a quip that no one reacted to there and then, but something that has stayed in my mind since and most likely always will.

Shortly after he laid his father to rest, Peter went for the biopsy on the mass in his leg. I was back in Norway when the call came through. Peter was relatively upbeat when he told me 'it's cancer me son'. He was matter of fact, and I believed even then he had been pretty sure what the results were going to show even before they came through. If I am being honest, I think that he had had a good idea as to what this small pea-sized lump might have been right back at the start but had lived in denial until this was no longer possible due to its increasing size.

Retinoblastoma, the cancer to which Peter lost his sight, is a rare form of childhood cancer and is caused by a mutation in the so-called

Retinoblastoma gene. As the mutation is present in all the body cells, there is also a greater risk of malignant growths developing elsewhere in the future. Peter had already lost two of his friends to cancer, both early sufferers of retinoblastoma and both suffering from other forms of cancer in their mid to late forties. It appeared that this too was the case with Peter.

Peter went on to tell me it was something called spindle cell sarcoma, and that as far as he knew the tumour in his calf was the only symptom. He was already booked in for a meeting with a consultant at The Royal Marsden Hospital in London.

The Marsden was founded in 1851 and was the first hospital in the world specializing in cancer treatment; the hospital was granted its Royal Charter in 1991 for the research work that it carried out. He was in excellent hands. Throughout all that was going on, Peter, the eternal optimist, was still talking about how great it would be to get back on skis, to go for a run and generally train. He was highly optimistic and was sure that this was just another small setback, and that he would beat this one too.

Spindle cell sarcoma is a type of connective tissue cancer in which the cells are spindle-shaped when examined under a microscope. Spindle cell sarcomas develop from connective tissue, a general term to describe fibrous tissue that connects and supports other tissues. The natural course of a spindle cell sarcoma would be to begin as a small swelling that continues to increase in size.

At first the lump will be self-contained and will not necessarily expand beyond its lump-like form. However, it may develop into something cancerous that can only be detected through microscopic examination. As such, the tumour is usually treated by excision that includes wide margins of healthy-looking tissue, followed by thorough biopsy and additional excision if necessary.

The prognosis for a tumour that is removed in the early stages is usually fairly positive, but if the tumour remains untreated and develops into the further stages of the disease, the prognosis is less good because the tumour cells are likely to spread to other locations. These locations can either be nearby tissues or system-wide locations that include the lungs, kidneys and liver. The latter stages are not always operable and will require chemotherapy and/or radiation treatment.

There is no hard and fast reason why spindle cell sarcoma develops; it can do so for a variety of reasons, including genetic predisposition, and it is highly likely that the retinoblastoma suffered in childhood left Peter predisposed for cancer in later life. It may also be caused by a combination of other factors, including injury and inflammation in patients that are already thought to be predisposed to such tumours. Spindle cells are a naturally occurring part of the body's response to injury. In response to an injury, infection, or other immune response, the connective tissues will begin dividing to heal the affected area.

I think the question on everyone's lips at that stage was why? Peter did not smoke, he was health conscious for the most part, and was extremely fit. Could his injuries of a few years before been the underlying event that triggered the spindle cells to mutate into a cancerous state, or would this have happened anyway?

There is no scientific evidence to prove that a trauma of the nature that Peter had suffered a few years before can trigger the start of a sarcoma. Sarcomas are a rarer form of cancer then carcinomas, whilst injuries are commonplace in everyone, both for those with and without genetic predisposition and a history of cancer. Despite it all, it is highly likely that Peter suffered another a cruel twist of fate and it was just a coincidence that the cancer manifested itself in the same leg that was injured as few years before.

The meeting with the consultant surgeon at The Royal Marsden Hospital in London went well. The form of treatment needed was obvious and was scheduled within a week. The consultant knew what Peter did in regard to sport and the level at which he competed; and knew how important his training and competitions were to his life.

The agreed action was straightforward. He would remove the tumour, including a good margin around the area to ensure that there was no chance of loose rogue cells being missed. He would do his absolute best to reconstruct Peter muscles so that he would be able to continue training and competing, even though his physical level of exercise would be reduced owing to the large amount of muscle mass that would need to be removed from his calf.

Surgery went well, the tumour was totally removed, and the surgeon managed to reconnect tendons so that Peter would have around 90% of normal movement in his foot. This meant that, although he may walk, train and run with a slight limp, he would still be able to carry on what he loved most in life – skiing.

There followed a period of rehabilitation in April and May 2001 to allow Pete's leg to heal. We knew it would take time, and that there was no point in rushing it. This was not the same as a recovery period after a torn muscle. This was recovery from major surgery.

In the early part of January that year, not long after Sid's death and before Peter's diagnosis, I was out training, keeping in shape so that I would be able to run with Peter when he was better. It was cold, dark and wet; I was not concentrating and stepped on an upturned curb stone, in an area where a new university was being built. I turned the same ankle that had resulted in me not being able to compete anymore and fell. I was used to this; it happened, and as a rule I could get up, and put weight on it enough to hobble home. Not this time. Something was different, the entire lower part of my right leg hurt, the ankle immediately swelling up over the outside of my shoe. No one was walking nearby, and I slowly limped and crawled back home. Marit contacted our neighbour and off to hospital we went. The ankle had finally broken on the medial side, some 10 years after I had first injured it.

A follow-up examination in April showed that a bone fragment in my ankle had formed a false joint and this was impacting on the function of the ankle. The best course of treatment was to have it surgically removed. By this time Peter had also had his surgery; he was recovering, and we were in contact daily. Peter recovered from his surgery much faster than I did. I was not able to run for 6 months; Peter was already exercising by the end of May.

Peter had regular follow ups at The Royal Marsden as an outpatient to check the size of the surgical site and also to ensure that the entire tumour had been removed and that there was no reoccurrence. Through a series of scans and X-rays the medical staff looked carefully for the start of any other form of tumour. In late July 2001, Peter phoned to say it was over. The last set of scans he had undergone were clear, and he was cancer free. Everyone breathed a huge sigh of relief. He had beaten cancer again, for the second time in his remarkable life. Now to get back to skiing.

It put things into a kind of perspective for me. I was sitting at home, frustrated and angry that I could not run after what really was a small injury. Peter had just got his head down, fought and beat cancer for the second time. In hindsight it was a highly inspirational time and goes to show that the small day-to-day setbacks we face are nothing compared to what others go through. We all take our good health for granted, and do not appreciate how fast life can change and be turned on its head. It was a wake-up call for me. Life is ultimately short, and we need to grasp it with both hands and make it what we want it to be.

I was now determined to get back to running as soon as possible. I worked hard at my physiotherapy and started cycling on a stationary bike as much as I could. Progress was slow, and painful. But it was progress and by the end of October that year I was back taking short, slow runs. I had plans to travel to England with Sara and Marit early in 2002 and running with Pete was the ultimate goal.

Peter intended to attend the Winter Games in Salt Lake City later that year as a supporter for the British team. He was not ready to compete, having spent very little time training for the level he would need to be at in order to do so. There was no way he would participate in the games as an also ran, as a shadow of the feared competitor he was renowned to be. Either he was there with a chance to come away with a medal, or he was not going to compete.

He had competed at seven other games. He could use his vast experience to help others who were less experienced. Whether you were able bodied, or disabled in anyway, you would be nervous. This was after all the Olympics, the pinnacle of sporting achievement. He would aim to calm nerves, provide encouragement and help to motivate the team. In addition, he could use the time to train and generally enjoy his time on the snow. Prior to this he had a training trip planned to Alaska in the latter part of January 2002. He was looking forward to it. It was the first time he had been on skis since his operation, and it was a long time coming.

THE FINAL RACE – PETE'S SKI FOR LIFE

I never spoke to Pete while he was in Alaska; there was a time difference and seeing as he was only away for a week or so we would catch up when he returned home. He called a couple of days after he got back. Said he had enjoyed the trip and had taken part in a small race which he had won. He had given his trophy to a friend, John Novotny, who had recently been diagnosed with terminal cancer, and whose illness was progressing fast. Pete had known John for many years, training with and competing against him. They had both lost their sight at similar ages and in similar circumstances. They were friends first and foremost, and Pete thanked his lucky stars that his cancer had manifested itself in his calf, where it was visible and operable. John's had manifested itself in the lung and was at an advanced stage when it was diagnosed.

He said he did feel dreadfully tired, something that was very unlike him. He initially told me that he put this down to the trip, training, and altitude, but there was something else. I called him out on it. He admitted he had felt tight chested whilst he was training, tired afterwards, and tired the next day when he woke up. He was a little concerned, but there was nothing he could do right there and then. He had an appointment for a 6-month check-up a week or so later; he would take it up with them then. He was sure it was nothing, that he had just overexerted himself what with being on skis for the first time in a long time.

We kept in touch almost daily in the time preceding his appointment at the Marsden. He called the evening following his appointment, sounding less upbeat, and, although I had a feeling what he was going to say, the words he spoke were chilling. They hit me like a blow to the stomach, as if someone had reached into my chest and tied my heart in a knot:

Dave mate, it's back! The fucking cancer is back. It's in my lung.

He explained that the scans had revealed a shadow on the lung; it was not a massive tumour so was probably in the early stages and he thought that to all intents and purposes it was something he could beat. His initial exchange with the surgeon had been typically direct. He had told them to cut it out. In fact, take the whole lung. He only needed one of those anyway and taking the whole thing would minimize the risk of rogue cells spreading elsewhere.

Prior to the diagnosis Pete had booked a trip to visit Dag in Norway and get some more skiing done. He was ever the optimist that the Salt Lake City Olympics could be realized despite having the cancer diagnosis.

Dag was working most of the time but had managed to get a decent set of tracks made for Peter to train alone. He left the radio on by the front door to the house so that Peter would be able to find his way back and forth when Dag was not around.

Dag recalls:

Peter was understandably subdued about getting another cancer diagnosis, we all were. But his love for skiing was so strong and he really believed he would beat it, again.

What I remember mostly about Peter at that time was that he said and thought a lot. He thought about what he was dealing with again, and I think maybe for the first time there was a doubt in his mind as to whether or not he could go through it again.

It is common for a secondary site of spindle cell sarcoma to be in the lung. It is not a carcinoma, and does not affect the lymph glands, which meant that there was less chance of it spreading further throughout his body. It would seem that it had originally stemmed from the earlier sarcoma in his calf, but whether this was due to it being removed at such a late stage or not is speculative and we will never know. The treatment option of surgical removal of the tumour seemed to be good but when the doctors looked closer at the position of the tumour, they found it to be extremely close to the aorta, (the largest artery in the body). The risk of nicking the aorta during the operation was too high. If this were to happen, Peter could die there and then on the operating table; it was not a risk they were willing to take.

The recommendation was that Peter underwent a course of chemotherapy in the hope that it would reduce the mass of the tumour, giving easier access and making surgery viable. A further discussion would then be held as to the best course of treatment to be undertaken. Pete's view was clear. Take it out, all of it. Just get it out.

Chemotherapy started shortly afterwards. The treatment was with the drugs doxorubicin and ifosfamide, administered over a 3-day period with a 17-day rest cycle between. One cycle lasted 21 days, which meant that his treatment plan would be over 5 or more months. Regular monitoring would be carried out to check the efficacy of the treatment. It had been agreed that as soon as it was safe to operate surgery would take place. As with all chemotherapy treatments there could be side effects: Pete was tough and, despite suffering the loss of much of his remaining hair, soldiered on and tried to live his life the best he could. Running and training took a back seat. He would take these up again afterwards; now he needed to recover and get well.

We kept in contact as usual during those times when he was not actually in the hospital and he managed to work for a while until the chemotherapy made him too tired. It must have been around the third cycle of treatment that Peter noticed a stinging, burning sensation in his arm where the drip was connected. This was found to be due to the leakage of the chemotherapy drugs into the surrounding tissue (extravasation). The effects of extravasation are many, but it can potentially cause serious injury and permanent harm, such as death of the tissue.

Peter was being monitored throughout the treatment: the tumour mass was shrinking and there was high optimism that after a few more cycles surgery might be possible. Peter was more positive than I had heard him for a long time. He was winning yet another battle against a truly strong competitor, just as he had done twice before.

By this time Marit and I were expecting our second child. I had not been home to London for a while and had planned to take Sara, who was by now almost 3 years old, to visit her grandparents, and I would take the opportunity to see Peter during what he hoped would be his last cycle of treatment before they decided if an operation was possible. If nothing else, I would be able to sit and talk to him directly and not through the telephone. Sara and I were to travel on a Saturday and stay for a little less than a week.

As normal I spoke with Peter in the days leading up to my trip and his final round of therapy. I was going to borrow a car and make the drive into London to the Royal Marsden and then travel home the same evening. Peter told me he felt generally well; he was tired and a little nauseous but, on the whole, could not complain. The only thing he complained about was that he had been suffering some really bad headaches during the last few weeks. Again, this was attributed to the chemotherapy, and he accepted this; the chemo was doing exactly what they wanted it to do, and he would hopefully get a concrete date for an operation if that was deemed to be the best course of treatment in his particular case.

He sounded tired when I spoke to him that day. I was travelling a couple of days later, and as I said goodbye, he stopped me. Peter was an honest and earnest man; he was sensitive but not overly emotional, almost to a degree where he could sound arrogant. He spoke clearly, and said, 'Dave, mate don't worry about me. I am going to kick this bastard, and I was thinking, maybe we should have a crack at the Windsor again next year.' As he said goodbye, he said 'I love you my son', and hung up. These were to be the last words I ever heard from him; they are seared into my heart and mind forever and will never leave me.

I was working a short drive from my home in Norway the next day and was between customer visits when I sent a message to Peter's girlfriend at the time. I basically was wondering how Peter's head was that morning. It was a while before the reply that come through, and when it did it stopped me in my tracks. It was quite blunt, and the wording turned me to stone at the side of the road. It felt as if a cold icy hand had reached into my chest again and had frozen my heart to a solid lump.

'Hi Dave, Peter went into a coma last night and is not expected to recover', it read. My best friend was fighting for his life. I was not due to travel until the next day. I hoped the message was slightly exaggerated; the thought that Pete might die filled me with an unimaginable feeling of dread. I drove home; there was no way anymore work was getting done that day.

I tried to contact Pete's family without any luck, but, nevertheless, decided I was going to change my ticket and travel that day. I rang the airline directly and explained the situation as best as I could. I remember it oh so clearly: I was speaking to someone who appeared to have no compassion, a real jobsworth who said there was nothing they could do. I had booked a cheap ticket for the trip, and if I wanted to change the ticket it would cost me full price for Sara and me in the only available class left – business class. The cost was £1,100, not something immediately available to me. I rang my parents and explained; they understood but had no way of helping me.

The day ticked past, minutes turned to hours and all the time I kept thinking that no news was good news. Pete was holding on. Maybe, just maybe, if he could hold on until I got there. Maybe knowing I was there would give him enough of a boost to pull through. We had achieved a lot together, done a lot together, been through a lot together. We could damn well get through this together too.

During the day I had tried to get hold of people who knew Peter. I don't know why; maybe it was a subconscious thought that told me the more people that knew, the more chance it would help him. Maybe it was the fact that I personally needed to get rid of the ice still firmly embedded in my chest and share with other people what was happening.

The phone rang, it was a UK number and I was expecting the voice of either Peter's girlfriend or one of his family. Instead I was greeted by Jim, the father of a friend of mine with whom I had worked at Barking and Dagenham Council. He knew Peter well, had helped at the Karatethon some years earlier and often saw Peter at the pub. He was in as much shock as I was, and when I told him about the airline, offered to lend me the money for the flight. It was due to land at Heathrow at around 9.20 pm. I never accepted the loan, having decided it would be too late by the time I got to the UK and to my parents' house. I would wait until the next day and travel with Sara as planned, and head directly to the hospital as soon as was possible.

I phoned Peter's brother again, and this time got through. He was in a hurry; he had only dashed home for a very short period after having been at the hospital since around 2 o'clock that morning when

Pete was admitted. There was not much he could tell me. He didn't know much himself but said that it didn't look good. I remember asking him to tell Pete to hang on at least until the next day, to tell him I was on my way. His answer rings in my ears to this day: 'Dave, Pete's not going to see tomorrow mate', and once again the icy lump returned to my chest, my body froze, and I did not know what to do. All I could do was hope.

There was nothing more to do; I made sure that I had packed what was needed and went to bed. The phone rang at around 11.30 pm in Norway, and, in tears, his brother told me the news. It was over. One of the most inspirational people I had even known, the person who knew me better than I knew myself, with whom I had laughed and cried, and guided for the best part of half my life, had died. The details of what happened next are somewhat blurred even today. I remember being told that it had been around 9 pm in the UK (an hour behind Norway) when Peter had stopped breathing for himself. As far as I recall, he had still been fighting right to the end, his heart continuing for a good while before he was taken from us. Pete had lost his final race. He had lost his ski for life.

9

The Black Dog Returns

After putting the phone down, following the news about Peter's death, there was not much sleep for me that night. I lay uneasy, thinking, churning thoughts over and over in my head. Why had this happened to one of the kindest and most honest people I knew?

Every time I asked a question the same answer came seeping back into my mind. It was my fault. It must be my fault. My Black Dog that had been kept at bay since the first Windsor Half Marathon had returned, and now it had its teeth firmly sunk into me.

I could not help but believe that had I been more assertive with Peter when I saw the lump in his leg right back at the start, then maybe it would have been dealt with earlier. Should I have physically taken him to the doctor's or the hospital, instead of leaving him to his own devices; should I have been there for him more? I felt a turmoil of emotions, which I could not then, and really cannot even to this day, explain. I only know that I felt bad. Events after the funeral in England led only to a heightening of these feelings. Feelings that, despite everything people have said since, still niggle at me from time to time some 17 years after Peter's death.

We travelled to England as planned that Saturday morning, but it was not until the Monday that I was able to get to the funeral home. I was met by Pete's brothers and one of his nephews. We walked into a room where a coffin was standing and, looking down into it, the denial I had put up as a protective barrier since the previous Friday was removed in a single moment.

Pete was dressed in his Great Britain training suit, with his skis tucked down his side. He had on his ski hat, and ski shoes and lay there peacefully, truly looking as though he were sleeping. It was only the second time I had seen a loved one who had died. A wealth of feelings washed over me: a mixture of happiness that Pete was not suffering, feelings of pride that I had been totally privileged to share a large part of my life with him, and an immense feeling of loss and sorrow. There was no use in trying to deny anything anymore; Pete was there, in front of me.

I had written a card for him, the contents of which I pretty much remember to this day; they will remain with me forever but what I had written stays between me and Pete. I placed in his hand the Essex County bronze we had worked so hard to win only 8 years earlier. It was as much his as mine and I wanted him to have it.

Next to his right hand, where he would have held the guiding rope, I placed my guide's vest. The vest was a fluorescent dayglow yellow. I had bought it in order for us to be visible in races. It had the word 'Guide' on the back so as there could be no mistaking that we were a team. It was only ever used in guiding races; as we had become quite well known around the different events over the years, I guess you could call it our calling card.

Now that Pete had passed away, my own reasons for running had ceased to exist. I wanted Pete to know that I was and always would be his guide no matter what and it was only right that he should take the vest with him. For me there would be no more guiding, for me there would be no more running; I neither possessed the heart or desire to do so anymore. That particular chapter of my life was closed.

I spent that entire day at the funeral home with Pete; I didn't eat or drink, I just sat, spoke with Pete's nephew, and spoke to Pete. I told him about what was going on and told him over and over again that I was sorry I had not been there when he really needed me. Most of all, I told him that I loved him. I had never told him when he was alive; we had been amazing friends and shared a connection that many people never come to experience in their entire lives. We had run, we had been a team, we had shared the most amazing closeness and understanding. He knew me better than anyone else had ever known me, and, most likely, better than anyone ever will. We had to all intents and purposes taken things somewhat for granted, and I, for one, believed that he was indestructible. We had joked many times about still running together as pensioners. Fate had, however, decided that it had other plans.

The next morning, I drove to Heathrow Airport and collected Dag, one of Pete's Norwegian guides, who had come to attend the funeral. We headed straight to the funeral home and said our last tearful goodbyes to Peter. It was to be the last time we were allowed to see him. As we left both Dag and I kissed Pete on the forehead, sharing one last bit of contact with him. As we left the funeral home it was raining, and I personally felt as though I had stepped into a void where nothing was important anymore. I felt like an empty shell filled with confusion, fear and an immense loneliness.

We discovered that the venue for the funeral had been changed. It had originally been planned that the service would be held in the chapel in the cemetery where Peter was to be buried. It was the same chapel where the service had been held for Pete's mum Joan a few years before. News had travelled fast, and we found that Peter was held in such high regard for the part he had played in helping to put British blind winter sports on the map, that the chapel was not going to be big enough.

The next day was the day of the funeral. I collected some of Peter's friends at the station to drive them to the service, and the sight that met us there was astonishing. There were busloads of people arriving and I'm not over-exaggerating or speaking metaphorically here. There were literally coaches parked along the side of the road, from which people of all nationalities and race, able-bodied and disabled alike, all descended and went into the church to pay their respects to Pete.

The church was quite modern and large but even, so it was standing room only, with many people standing in the foyer area. The service passed by in somewhat of a cloud for me. I was shaking, felt weak, and despite my best efforts, cried like a baby for the entire service.

After the church service the funeral procession headed to the cemetery. As per tradition the other traffic stopped so that the procession could drive in convoy. Pete would have loved this: causing a traffic jam on a busy road, such were the numbers of cars and coaches.

The service had already started by the time a lot of mourners reached the graveside and I found this quite distressing. It stopped raining and the sun shone casting a bright shaft of light onto the coffin and the awnings that were around the grave. I am not sure why but seeing the coffin had driven me back into denial that it was not Pete but someone else who had died. I almost expected to hear his dulcet tones asking when it was time for the wake to start as he was parched.

The service came to an end and the coffin was lowered into the ground. As earth was thrown on the coffin, I heard nothing other than the sobs of Peter's friends and family trying so hard to stay composed whilst saying goodbye to someone who had touched the lives of so many. After the vicar commanded us to go in peace, people started to disperse. I found myself drawn to the graveside. I carried a white rose which I threw in a gentle arc on to the coffin. The noise it made as it landed seemed inexplicably loud, and as I stepped forwards I saw that it lay in a perfectly straight line on the coffin, with the crown petals just touching the bottom of the brass sign bearing Peter's name, date of birth and date of passing. The sun shone down directly on the grave, and I believe it was here that things really hit home. Pete was actually dead. He was not coming running anymore, and I would never speak to him again, at least not in this life.

I remember nothing more until I heard a voice shouting my name. I remember someone pulling at me and physically lifting me away from the grave. I never found out what happened, but my suit was dreadfully muddied, my hands filthy and the earth around the ground awnings beside the grave somewhat in disarray. It looked as though I had been digging, though no one ever told me what had happened.

The wake was held at the club where Pete and his friends often went for a beer at the weekends, and I had gone there fully intent on drowning my sorrows and leaving my car there until next day. I walked in, cleaned up as best I could and got a beer, before finding somewhere quiet where I could just sit and drink myself into a stupor. People around me were laughing and joking but I could not for the life of me see what there was to be happy about. Pete was dead. Or had they already forgotten him?

Someone, who shall remain nameless, came over and I was faced with a torrent of words that totally tore me apart. I was accused of deserting Peter when I moved to Norway, of ruining his career, of breaking his heart, and of not giving him a reason to fight harder against the cancer that claimed him because I was not there for him when he needed me most.

These comments, exactly the same as the thoughts that I had encountered in my own mind after Peter had died, ripped through me; hot tears fell down my face, and I left the wake. It was the last time I saw many of the people from the visually impaired world that I had been a part of for the best part of 20 years. I had only drunk a mouthful of beer; I jumped into the car basically not caring anymore and drove to the only place that I could think of, the only place that allowed me to be with Pete alone for a while. To the forest where we had run countless miles every week for almost the entire time we ran together.

I parked and, ignoring the wet muddy ground and the fact that I had a suit and dress shoes on, just walked. I must have walked round and round for a couple of hours before the blisters caused by the shoes made it impossible to go any further. I drove home and said nothing to anyone. I just wanted to be left alone with my thoughts, to try to make sense as to what had been said to me, and, more to the point, why it had been said. But, most of all, I needed to try and find out whether all the things I was accused of had an ounce of truth in them, and whether me moving away had ultimately destroyed Pete's will to continue fighting.

Sara and I travelled back to Norway the next day. It was quite hectic, what with having to take the tube, and with baggage and a 3-year-old; a 3-year-old who was naturally excited to be going home to her mum, a mum whose stomach was rapidly growing larger.

Once we got on board the plane Sara went to sleep almost immediately, leaving me to sit and ponder. Sitting alone on the plane my only thoughts were of the vitriolic words that had been used to attack me whilst I was possibly at the lowest point of my life.

No matter how I tried to make sense of it, no matter how I tried to soften their impact, the same thoughts came back to me. It was my fault. It had to be my fault. Pete was dead because I had left him, breaking his heart and giving him nothing to fight with anymore.

Returning back to Norway other events made it impossible for me to dwell on these thoughts for too long. I was back at work the next day and then there were preparations for the new baby. I was done with running, so I packed all my running stuff into boxes and hid them away in the loft. I also decided to cut all contact with Mick Brace, Jimmy Denton, Kenny Bodden and the others in the UK and also with Dag, Pete's guide in Norway, with whom I had discussed so many times the areas where Peter needed strengthening in order to be the best he could be for his competitions. All numbers were deleted from my mobile phone and the pages of the address book ripped out. The names, addresses, contact details and all memories associated with them were hidden away somewhere in my subconscious.

Furthermore, the troubling thoughts that I had been an accessory to Pete's passing because of my 'abandonment' of him, along with the memories of the time Pete and I had spent together, were also buried deep inside my mind. It was the only way that I felt I could cope, and although Pete was always with me the pain I felt did fade, as did my desire to run, and train.

However, through various events all happening at the same time, the Pandora's box buried in my mind started to creak at the hinges. In 2013 I received a copy of Sebastian Coe's autobiography as a Christmas present, I read it cover to cover and could remember running sessions similar to those described with Peter. Of the other coincidence that awakened something in me was seeing a photo of Peter and me running the Windsor Half Marathon in 1995. In a couple of years' time it would be 20 years since that race. I decided that I had to run again.

I completed the race, I had done what I wanted to do, run the half marathon exactly 20 years after the first time I had run it with Peter. I ran in the memory of Peter and raised money for CLIC Sargent, a charity dealing with helping families of children suffering with cancer to be there for their children.

My thinking was that completing the race 20 years after running it the first time would allow me to banish the ghosts of the past. Pandora, though, had other ideas. A number of coincidences again a few years later ripped the box wide open, spilling its contents into my brain, in exactly the same unsorted mess that I had packed them all those years earlier. With a little persuasion, a large push and a heck of a lot of support I have managed to sort the jumble of thoughts, memories and pain into some semblance of order, the result being this book.

Finally, Peter's story is at least here in part. A truly remarkable man, competitor, opponent and most of all friend who inspired everyone he met. A man who took the hand of cards that fate had given him and played a hard game in return, before he was cruelly and untimely taken away from us all. He may be gone from us in the physical world, but he will live on always in those of us who were lucky enough to have had him in their lives.

A million times I've needed you

A million times I've cried

If love alone

Could have saved you Pete

You would never have died

In life you were loved dearly

In death I love you still

In my heart you hold a space

Where no one can ever fill

It broke my heart to lose you

But you didn't go alone

Part of me went with you Pete

The day God took you home

Always your guide.

About the Author

Dave was born in Romford Essex in 1971 and like most boys of the time wanted to be a professional footballer. When he started secondary school he noted that he was a half decent runner and with the encouragement of a teacher joined Newham and Essex Beagles Athletics club, aged 12. He juggled between playing football and running before deciding it was running he liked best.

Through school he worked voluntarily with the handicapped for some years, and when he was introduced to Peter Young and the world of visually handicapped sport, he became totally consumed in it. His own running improved massively and he developed a great friendship with someone whom was to become a mentor in many ways, including the ways of life.

Dave moved to Norway in 1997 and returned to the UK in 2019. He is currently working in Tetbury Gloucestershire within his second love, the field of health and safety at work.